YOUR
ANGEL
JOURNEY

First published by O Books, 2008
O Books is an imprint of John Hunt Publishing
Ltd., The Bothy, Deershot Lodge, Park Lane,
Ropley, Hants, SO24 0BE, UK
office1@o-books.net
www.o-books.net

Distribution in:

UK and Europe
Orca Book Services
orders@orcabookservices.co.uk
Tel: 01202 665432 Fax: 01202 666219 Int. code
(44)

USA and Canada
NBN
custserv@nbnbooks.com
Tel: 1 800 462 6420 Fax: 1 800 338 4550

Australia and New Zealand
Brumby Books
sales@brumbybooks.com.au
Tel: 61 3 9761 5535 Fax: 61 3 9761 7095

Far East (offices in Singapore, Thailand, Hong
Kong, Taiwan)
Pansing Distribution Pte Ltd
kemal@pansing.com
Tel: 65 6319 9939 Fax: 65 6462 5761

South Africa
Alternative Books
altbook@peterhyde.co.za
Tel: 021 555 4027 Fax: 021 447 1430

Text copyright Joylina Goodings 2008

Design: Stuart Davies
Front cover picture by Adrian Holland
www.amazola.com
Line drawings by Nicola Woodham

ISBN: 978 1 84694 104 7

A CIP catalogue record for this book is available
from the British Library.

Printed by CPI Antony Rowe, Chippenham, UK

O Books operates a distinctive and ethical publishing philosophy in
all areas of its business, from its global network of authors to
production and worldwide distribution.
This book is produced on FSC certified stock, within ISO14001
standards. The printer plants sufficient trees each year through
the Woodland Trust to absorb the level of emitted carbon in
its production.

To Anastasi

Enjoy

YOUR
ANGEL
JOURNEY

love light & Angel wings

Joylina Goodings

BOOKS

Winchester, UK
Washington, USA

CONTENTS

Preface   1

Part One - The Beginning   5

Chapter 1 – History of Angels   5
The Angel Hierarchy   6
Fallen Angels   8
What are Angels?   9
Difference between Angels & Spirit Guides   10
Opening to Angels   11
Protecting Yourself with the Angels   13

Chapter 2 – Angels and Ritual   15
Creating an Angel Altar or Sacred Space   15
How to Ask the Angels for Help   17
Getting the Answers   20
Symbols and Dreams   22
Angel Cards   27

Chapter 3 – Chakras and Auras   29
The Body's Energy System   29
The 7 Major Chakras   29
Chakra opening   34

Chapter 4 – Healing   38
What is Universal Healing Energy?   38
What is the Purpose of Healing?   38
What is Healing?   39
Connecting to Archangel Raphael's Healing Energy   42
Spirit Guides   44
Things to Remember Before Meditative Journey Work   46
How to Interpret your Journeys   47

Journey to Meet your Spirit Guide 51

Visualisation 52

Guardian Angels 57

Dreams 58

The Fifth Dimension 59

Journey to Meet your Guardian Angel 60

Part II – Your Journey

Chapter 5 – Sandolphon 64

Starting 64

Root Chakra (one) 65

Connecting to Archangel Sandolphon 68

Replenishing Earth Energy 71

Sending Healing to Troubled Areas on the Planet 72

Chapter 6 – Phuel 73

The Sacrum Chakra (two) 74

Connecting to Archangel Phuel 78

Chapter 7 – Uriel and Ramaela 82

The Solar Plexus Chakra (three) 82

Clearing the Solar Plexus with Archangel Uriel 87

Connecting to Archangel Ramaela 92

Chapter 8 – Chamuel 94

The Heart Chakra (four) 94

The Heart 97

Breathing in Peace Meditation 98

Connecting to Archangel Chamuel 102

Chapter 9 – Gabriel, Michael, and Zadkiel 107

Throat Chakra (five) 111

Journey to Archangel Michael and Archangel Gabriel 114

Mantras   118
Letting Go of Past Life Vows with Archangel Zadkiel   119
Visualisation   121
Inner listening   122

Chapter 10 – Zagzagel   **124**
Brow Chakra ~ known as the Third Eye (five)   124
Intuition, Balance, Masculine & feminine   125
Clairvoyance, Clairaudience, Clairsentience, Claircogniscence   127
Connecting to your Inner Vision with Archangel Zagzagel   128

Chapter 11 – Melchisadec   **130**
Crown Chakra   130
About Archangel Melchisadec   132
Visualisation   133
Choices & Indecisiveness   136
Letting Go of Addictions with Archangel Uriel   140
Balancing Masculine and Feminine Energies with Metatron
    and Shekinah   141

Chapter 12   **144**
The Pentagram of Angels   144
Techniques for Balancing & Clearing Chakras   146
How to Know if you are Blocked   146
Visualisation with Light   146
Toning   147
Increasing Confidence   147
Spiritual Growth   149

Further Reading   151
Recommended Music   152
Visualization CDs   152
Angel Cards   152

ACKNOWLEDGEMENTS

Many people have contributed to the writing of this book and it is difficult to know where to start. Firstly I would like to thank my parents for giving me the life I chose and asked for on a soul level for without this learning I would not have been writing this at all.

To Geoff and Eileen for originally expressing their faith in me and being instrumental in changing the way I looked at myself and my life.

To all the people along my journey, teachers, counsellors, friends, students and clients all of whom touched my heart and gave me courage and faith in myself. Who shared their love and wisdom. Especially to Ali who kindly read and edited the first draft of this book and without whose encouragement I would most probably never have approached a publisher. To O'Books for taking me on.

To my children Nicole and Stephen for supporting me and being proud of me even when they thought I was going mental. Above all to Graham without whose unconditional love, support, encouragement and total acceptance of me as I am, I would never have had the courage to start this journey.

And last but not least to the angels themselves for waiting so patiently for me to be ready to allow them into my life and for guiding me with their unconditional love to start the process of identifying and letting go my baggage and giving me the courage to live my joy and share that love with others.

Preface

This book is more than an introduction to angels, more than an explanation of how to work with them. It's a journey into yourself as well as into their world. It will show you how to heal yourself, connect to your soul's purpose and change your life so that you can be all that you want to be.

Work with the exercises that have helped me and many others find our spiritual path, our true selves. They will change you. The changes might be dramatic, or slow and gentle, or deep, subtle ones that you struggle to notice, but they will come. They will bring you inner security and contentment, according to your own will and needs.

I felt guided in writing this book, but it wasn't until I was finishing that I thought of the obvious question – *who was doing the guiding?* I closed my eyes and meditated for a few moments and after a while I received a name. It sounded like "Ithuriel". I rushed to my copy of the *Dictionary of Angels* but couldn't find an Ithuriel anywhere. Disappointed, I returned to my meditation to reconnect and find out more. The energy was certainly there, teasing and gentle. All it said was that I would find out about him very soon. So, trusting, I finished my meditation and said thank you.

I got up and was drawn to Angela McGerr's book, The Book of Angels, within the Gold & Silver Guardian Angels set. It opened naturally at – guess what – Ithuriel, and with Angela's kind permission, this is what I read:

"Ithuriel – Guardian Angel of Your True Self".

"If invoked from the heart I show you the person that you really want to be, but perhaps have imprisoned for the moment. It is time to release your inner self from behind the bars you have erected, and embrace truth and freedom."

And this of course is exactly what this book is about: connecting to your true self.

The message of Ithuriel is that he can show you the person you are really meant to be. You may have lost it. It may be hidden from you right now, under layers of self-protection. Why is the real you behind bars of your own creation? He can help you let go of these layers, one by one, and truly be yourself. It is not an easy journey. But with Ithuriel's help and that of the other angels, you can succeed. It just takes perseverance, determination and being kind and gentle with yourself. The more you love and respect yourself, the more others will love and respect you, and the happier and more fulfilled you will be.

We are all on our own journeys of transformation and there are many different routes. This is just one. Some things in this book will resonate with you and you'll get much from them. Those that don't, just leave them. You might come back to them later. All the exercises can be used over and over again, taking you through to new and deeper understandings and awakenings. This journey will lead you wherever you wish it to. Wherever you and your guardian angel have already pre-planned to be. This is just the beginning… or perhaps, the beginning of the next stage.

Imagine you are a caterpillar starting to spin a chrysalis. What are you doing, you are protecting yourself but why? It makes no sense, but you know you must do it. As a chrysalis, the DNA and molecules inside you are all being mixed up and re-organised but you don't know why, your life is either falling apart or you just feel the need to move on. You know you can no longer be a carefree caterpillar. There is something else, but what? This is the journey, to become a butterfly. But don't worry too much. The caterpillar doesn't wonder what it is going to be. Nor does it try to ensure it becomes a Royal Emperor rather than a Meadow Sweet. Does it worry about whether it should be a moth? Of course not, it just allows the transformation and emerges as its true, beautiful self in its own time. This is the journey we will be taking together in this book. Allow yourself to see, sense and feel the butterfly you already are then share it with the world.

Take it slowly. There is no rush, your journey is the journey of your whole life. Give yourself time to notice, to absorb, to grow. The tree that grows too fast collapses under its own weight, the roots don't go deep enough to stop it being blown over in a gale.

Your body needs time to assimilate the new energies and frequencies you encounter.

We always seem to be rushing from A-to-B, whether on planes or fast-track careers. But the journey of our life is best explored and treasured on a day-by-day basis. Why cross the country on the interstate or motorway of your life, and miss out on all the sights and the beautiful countryside along the way? We spend our time reliving the past or worrying about the future, rather than in the only real bit of life; the life we are living right now. Let's start by taking things in, savouring the beauty of everything around us, our place in it, ourselves, and each other.

This book is comprehensive, but with such a rich subject we can't cover everything in detail, so there's a recommended reading list at the back. We will be working with our body's energy centres known as chakras, as well as with angels. We will be using colour, crystals and aromas. We will be using creative visualisation exercises. Writing, drawing and reflection during this work are all useful and it would be helpful to record your experiences. You'll need a book or journal to write in, coloured pencils, pens, or paints to help you to capture the feelings. You don't need to be an artist or be able to draw well. I certainly can't, I use abstract form and colour. I'm not always sure about what I experience, I just start, and my hand seems to have a mind of its own. I have learned to just trust the process and know that what needs to come out, will come out. Doing this will help you express your feelings, to see how far you have come in your journey. Notice the little steps you have taken, the little successes, because they can add up to a big change. I'll be recounting stories and examples from my own life and journey to help explain the process.

With some exercises later it can be helpful to read the exercise onto a tape recorder so you don't need to be distracted during the exercise itself. Or you can purchase the accompanying CDs from my website – www.joylina.com

I wish you joy on your journey.

Joylina

PART I THE BEGINNING

CHAPTER 1

History of Angels

The word angel comes from the Greek angelos, and means messenger. It is a translation of the Hebrew word mal'akh.

Angels have been around since the beginning of time. They have never been human. They are an energy created by the Divine / Creator (God / Goddess – or however you like to address this being or energy. Defining your God is not within the parameters of this book but there are some recommendations for further reading at the end should you wish to explore further.) Angels were created at the creation of the universe to act as an intermediary between the Creator and ourselves.

The earliest recorded references to angels, depicting them as winged human-like creatures, are as long ago as 3000 BC as stone carvings and statues in the Sumerian culture. Winged messengers appear in myths and legends of most early cultures, Egyptian (Horus), Mayan, Greek (Hermes), Roman (Mercury) Indian and Chinese. References to winged messengers appear in all the current religions as well including Christianity, Buddhism, Judaism, Hinduism, and Islam. All current religious texts have references to winged messengers from God to us.

Just because earlier cultures did not leave physical evidence does not mean there was no culture or belief in angels. Almost certainly, the motif of a winged human figure goes back much further into the shamanic cultures around the world. Recently I even saw an angel figure painted in some South African bushman rock art that is dated between 6-10 thousand years old. Even today shamanic belief and practices have survived across the world from Tibet to Siberia, Lapland to North and South America, Europe to Australia and New Zealand. In most shamanic practices it is believed the shaman flies through time and space in trance to the spirit world to connect to the souls of his/her clients.

The Angel Hierarchy

In Roman times a priest sorted the angels into a hierarchy of 9 that has since been a commonly held belief.

Seraphim, Cherubim, Thrones ~ the Heavenly Counsellors and closest to God
Dominions, Virtues, Powers ~ Heavenly Governors
Principalities, Archangels, Angels ~ Heavenly Messengers

I personally do not accept there is a hierarchy, as we would know it. This feels like a human invention to me. Especially as some of the major archangels are also known to work on other levels, such as Archangel Uriel Angel of the North and one of the four major archangels charged with protecting the universe, who is also a Throne. So perhaps it is a less hierarchical structure, like the matrix management that is currently in vogue, maybe it is "as on earth so as it is in heaven".

In the Kabbalah there are ten levels and their names are **Foundation, Splendour, Eternity Beauty, Power, Grace, Knowledge, Wisdom, Understanding and Perfection**. This is often portrayed as a tree, the tree of life. At the root stands Sandolphon who extends through the tree into the universe. Other angels appearing on the tree are Saphkiel, angel of contemplation, Raphael, Gabriel, Michael, Uriel, and Metatron plus three others who vary according to what you are reading. We will be learning more about all these angels later.

Below is a brief description of the various angelic levels that are currently commonly accepted, as decreed by the priests in Roman times.

Seraphim ~ The Seraphim are considered the highest order. They are highly evolved beings and closest to God. They balance the movement of the planets, stars and the heavens by using sound.

Cherubim ~ These are the Guardians of Light that comes from the energy within the stars. Their name stands for wisdom and they are the guardians and record-keepers of the heavens.

Thrones ~ These are the angels of the planets. Each planet has its own

Throne; the guardian of our planet Earth (Ghia) is known as the Earth angel. In the Old Testament (Ezekiel I) they are described as having four faces and four wings.

Dominions ~ These are the regulators of all the angelic beings who are not as evolved as themselves. Their purpose is to advise the less evolved angelic groups. They have been depicted as carrying golden staffs in their right hand and the seal of God in their left hand.

Virtues ~ These are often referred to as the "shining ones" since they transmit enormous beams of divine light. They are believed to be the Angels of Blessings. The two angels present at the Ascension of Jesus are believed to have been virtues.

Powers ~ They protect our souls from the lesser energies in the world. The powers are the keepers of the Akashic records (the records of all the thoughts and deeds of each soul's evolutionary journey). Archangel Metatron is thought to be the head keeper of these records and is one of the few humans who ever attained angelhood. The prophet Enoch was supposed to have been transformed into an angel by God in recompense for his devotion during his many lifetimes. The Powers oversee birth, death and rebirth. The only other human who is said to have been transformed by God into an Angel is the prophet Elijah who became Archangel Sandolphon who is responsible for grounding and anchoring positive energies into the Earth and transforming negative energies.

Principalities ~ They oversee large groups and organisations. They are believed to guard nations, cities and leaders. The angel who helped David when he killed Goliath is thought to be from this order.

Archangels ~ Archangel Gabriel is Angel of the West, of the element of water, in charge of communication, who brought Mary and Joseph the news of Jesus' coming. He also is thought to have communicated to Muhammad the whole basis of the Koran and what subsequently became the Muslim faith. Archangel Michael, Angel of the South, of the element of fire, is the warrior angel of truth, courage and protection. It is believed to be Archangel Michael who appeared during World War 1 as the Angel of Mons. Archangel Raphael, Angel of the East, of the element of air, is responsible for healing, science and knowledge, and leads all the healing angels. Archangel Uriel, Angel of the North, of the element of earth, oversees giving and receiving, and as the Angel of the Earth is also a Throne.

Angels ~ These are those closest to us and include everyone's guardian angels. There are many different kinds of angels within this group with many different purposes, such as bringers of joy, hope, healing, peace, laughter, self-acceptance, forgiveness.

The Jewish sacred text, the Talmud, says that every blade of grass has an angel.

Angels are the highest form of energy that come from the elemental kingdom which also consists of all the nature spirits including faeries, devas, sylphs, sprites, salamanders, elves, and (undines). Nature spirits were widely believed in by all the Semitic peoples of the Middle East as they still are in many shamanic cultures.

Fallen Angels

This section would not be complete if I did not mention Fallen Angels. Zoroastrianism that began in the Middle East between the fourth and second millennia before Christ, according to records, first seemed to introduce negative energies. They had many angels including a Lord of Light. To create balance, there was a Lord of Darkness with his demons and evil spirits. In the first instance, the demons of Zoroastrianism, were referred to as devas. In modern thought, devas are an elemental nature spirits working for good.

Many Zoroastrianism beliefs were incorporated into Judaism with more and more angels finding their way into Jewish writings which became the basis for many current religions. People migrated through the Middle East at this time and in and out of India and China, and various beliefs travelled and intermingled. This does not explain how these similar beliefs appear in shamanic cultures on different continents.

The leader of Hebrew forces of evil Aka Shedim, was also known as Satan the Antagonist. Belial, the spirit of perversion, darkness and destruction; Mastema, enmity or opposition. Other darker angels appear in the Torah (which forms the first five books of the Christian Old

Testament), these include Azazel – demon of the wilderness, and Lilith – a female demon of the night. There are many more but they are not the subject of this book. The full story of the fall of the group of angels known as the Watchers can be found in the Old Testament Book of Enoch.

What are Angels?

Angels are energy; they dwell in the fifth to seventh dimensions and their vibrational frequency is higher than humans who live in a third dimensional world. This is why we can't see them. They are genderless beings, made up of an equal balance of male and female energy. They are completely androgynous, which is why some people experience them differently, some as male, others as female. They resonate unconditional love. They have never incarnated in human form (except where mentioned) and they never will. Neither will we ever become angels. This does not stop angels using humans to do things for them, which is why we often see people as angels. "You're an angel," we say as someone helps us. As we develop and become more aware of our spiritual selves our vibrations rise and we can begin to connect to our spirit guides and angels.

There are so many angels. There is an angel for everything. As many angels as our imaginations can create. They represent archetypal energies. They have been around so long and been called so many different things in so many cultures and languages, I don't think it matters what you call them. As long as you know the quality of the energy you are asking for in your life, the appropriate angel will come. You can call the Archangel of Healing, Communication, Creativity. You don't have to remember their names.

We each have our own guardian angel who is appointed to watch over us, look after us, journey with us throughout our many lifetimes. We have the same guardian angel though all our incarnations. This angel knows us inside out, our strengths, our weaknesses, our soul essence. We can keep nothing from them and they love us unconditionally. They hold the overview of our soul's journey through the many lifetimes we lead. They are with us from the time our soul incarnates until it should decide to stop journeying or when it rejoins the Source.

You and your guardian angel can ask all the other angels to assist you as and when you need them.

People usually sense angels and guides but some will also see them in their mind's eye, or hear them as a voice in their head. You may also encounter them in dreams and in meditation. Sometimes they appear as golden, silver or violet orbs of light in your peripheral vision, darting quickly across space.

Angels evolve by serving humans so you are helping them, as well as yourself, by inviting them into your life. Universal Divine law says angels can't help us unless we ask them to so you do have to invite them in and ask them for assistance and guidance. You also need to listen to their answers. Asking them is easy, you just pray. Angels read what's in your heart not what's in your mind so as long as you are praying from your heart you will be heard. Hearing their responses is more difficult and they come in many ways, during meditation, in music, as a message read in magazines or books, or encounters with people. We will be going into this in more detail later.

The Difference Between Spirit Guides and Angels

Spirit Guides are human energy and have had many lifetimes. They are wise loving people. They continue evolving on the spirit side by agreeing to assist us in our lives in whatever way they can. They offer guidance, inner knowledge and inner peace, love and wisdom, but they will not and cannot make your choices for you. You have free will. You are the creator of your life and only you can choose your path. They can help you reach your full potential. They can show you the direction of your life and help in many practical ways with this lifetime.

Spirit Guides have differing experiences and responsibilities so although you'll have one guide who is often referred to as the "doorkeeper", you'll also have other guides helping you with differing phases of your life depending upon your needs at any particular time, for practical, emotional, spiritual guidance.

Each individual's soul growth depends upon wisdom and love gained during their many lifetimes and the vibrational level the person is operating at. As you raise your vibrational levels whilst working through this book so the vibrations of your guide rise too. You help each other in your evolution. You also start to work with the higher guides and grand masters. The more experiences we have and the more we accept ourselves as we are and become the best that we can be, the higher our vibration goes.

We live and work in the third dimension. Our bodies vibrate at this level. When we relax, go into trance, meditate or sleep, the vibration of our body raises to the fourth dimensary level. This is where many spirit guides operate, and this is the level where most people's loved ones are. It is the closest to us. As we deepen our trance and become more evolved as beings, we can access the higher vibrations such as the fifth, sixth and seventh dimensions. Within each dimension there are many differing levels of vibration, which is why you'll sense the different types of energies of the different guides and angels.

Angels are pure energy. They operate between the fifth and seventh dimensions, and maybe beyond. Seven dimensions, seven heavens, are well recognised but the field of science and quantum physics is constantly changing and many people now believe there are an infinite number of dimensions. As such we need to raise our vibrations to connect to them and you'll be doing this as you go through this book.

Opening to Angels

Much has been written about opening to angels. Everyone has his or her own unique way of doing so. What's important is that whatever you do feels natural and comfortable for you. Angels naturally answer you and draw nearer when you speak to them. You do not have to do it out loud, in your head will do. They are influenced by the power of your intention. Performing some sort of ritual can add power to that intention, if you feel comfortable with ritual. If you don't it is not necessary, although meditation and all forms of focussing can be interpreted as ritual. We will be discussing ritual in more detail later.

Under universal law, angels are not allowed to interfere in your life unless invited to by you. Nor can they do anything that is not for your highest good and the highest good of all others concerned. They are not allowed to interfere in your karma in any way but they can guide you through whatever issues you came into this life to face and the learning experiences you encounter, giving you love, support and confidence that you are not alone.

Your own personality, life experience and make up will determine how you wish to approach opening to angels. I was extremely sceptical at first. Not because I didn't believe they existed; I had seen one and experienced its energy more than once in my life, (my mother said I could not possibly have seen an angel, I was not good enough and to stop telling lies). But rather, "Why would they bother with little insignificant me?" Before I actually asked my guardian angel for anything, or even a sign it was there, I asked for the car parking angel to find me a parking space. I noticed I started finding spaces much more easily and that whichever car park or road I went to someone was always just leaving, so I started to have more faith in the fact they might indeed notice me amongst all those other worthier souls out there. This book sets out the tools and techniques I used for myself and others to overcome my lack of self worth, define my life, and move and continue to move into who I am meant to be.

Working with angels can bring about dramatic change in your life, not only on the outside but also on the inside. It is the inside that changes first. This then allows the outside of your life to change. If I am worthy enough to get parking spaces then maybe I am worthy enough to ask for other things as well. In fact after receiving the proof I needed my experience changed. I began to notice changes inside myself which enabled the changes on the outside of my life to take place. I had to feel worthy and confident in myself before I could give up the day job and work with the angels as my sole source of income. After all I had two children to support at the time.

Once you have invited the angels into your life you'll begin to see the signs of their help. One of the first signs you might encounter will be finding white feathers. These may be small, they may be large, and they may come just to comfort you and to tell you your angel is there. They might come before a big decision pointing out that you will be given a sign to help you make the decision, or they may come after you have made your choice or come to a new insight, praising you so you know you have got it right. Remember when you see a white feather it is there for a reason, just because it came out of your duvet or pillow after a bad nightmare does not mean it has no significance. There are many more brown feathers in your duvets and pillows than white ones. Angels use many methods to communicate with us and we shall discuss these in more detail later. You'll also develop your own unique ways as you learn to interpret the signs yourself.

Protecting yourself with Angels

Angels are all loving beings and so there is no reason to fear them. But many people do fear things they can't explain and are afraid they might come under some sort of negative attack. This has never happened to me, or anyone I know, in all my years of working with angels. However the following exercise will also protect you from physical harm, if it is for your highest good.

Exercise

This is a very quick and simple exercise to do. It can be done anywhere, anytime, but I suggest that you settle yourself in a space where you feel safe and comfortable. You can put on some soft soothing music; burn some incense or aromatherapy oil. Anything you like will do but frankincense is good. *(When burning incense or candle do ensure they are safe and never left unattended).*

Settle yourself comfortably and close your eyes. Concentrate on your breathing. Breathe slowly and deeply and imagine that with every out breath you are letting go of all your every day problems and you are becoming more and more relaxed.

Invite your guardian angel to come close to you, to open its wings and totally surround you. Encompassing your whole body. Over your head and under your feet as well. Imagine this happening, feel the wings expanding and surrounding you.

Know that only positive loving energy can pass through this protection.

Know that any negative energy from people or spirit will be absorbed and transformed into loving energy and returned to where it came from with angelic love and healing. Know that nothing, not even you're worst fears can harm you while you have these wings around you.

Make this as real for yourself as possible. Use your creative imagination and all your senses. Your imagination is the creative part of you that connects you to the creator of all things.

Now write down in your journal your experiences from this meditation. You may even want to draw something. You don't need to be a writer or an artist to capture the feelings you just experienced. Any abstract form using different colours will capture the essence of your experience and reveal hidden depths to the experience, you may not have been consciously aware of at the time.

You can use the same meditation to call any angel to you. Instead of invoking your guardian angel you can, for example, invoke Archangel Michael, the angel of truth, courage and protection. His wings are bright blue and he carries a golden sword so nothing and no one can harm you. If you wish to use ritual to enhance your energy and intention then call his name three times, "Archangel Michael, Archangel Michael, Archangel Michael, please draw near me and protect me and let me feel your wings around me. Only positive energy can pass through your wings any negative energy is transmuted to positive loving energy and returned to wherever it came from." He is the mighty warrior angel but more of him later. Remember to write down or draw your experiences and notice the different energies.

CHAPTER 2

Angels and Ritual

Angels do like ritual but it is not necessary. You can call an angel to your side by being honest with yourself. If you are asking (praying) from your heart they will hear and answer. It is your intention that is important. So if you are not comfortable working with ritual you don't need to, they will still be there, protecting you and bringing you what you need for your highest good.

If you do enjoy ritual then it adds power to your intention. Some people say that if you use an ancient ritual it will be more powerful because it contains the power of the intentions of all the people who have used it in the past. This may be true but you can never be sure how it was used in the past. Many people have misused their powers in past lives and it often puts them off using ritual again in this life. Also, the ritual is someone else's. It may have felt good to them but it may not feel right for you. If you are uncomfortable don't do it. I always feel it is better to create your own rituals.

It is important you are comfortable with what you are doing and therefore creating your own ritual will contain more of your intent and will help you in bringing to you what you need for your highest good. Remember it is detachment from the result that brings you what you most need in your life.

When calling an angel I usually say their name or quality three or four times. It can be done in your mind or out loud. I have also felt the energy when I have done nothing. I do whatever I am guided to do on any particular day. It is up to you. It works on the power of your intention, not what you do or how you do it.

Creating an Angel Altar or Sacred Space

Creating an angel altar is one way of letting the angels know you are ready and wish to work with them. This can be done by setting aside a whole room for yourself or just setting aside a box containing the things you wish to use. The advantage of a box is you can carry it about with you and use it wherever you will. I have a shelf in my bedroom laid out where I can perform rituals, ask and listen, whenever I wish. I also carry certain things in a bag so I can create an altar wherever I am working. I also have representative items in the corners of my home, making my whole home an altar.

You can put anything you like on your altar because you are creating it for yourself. You can use pictures representing angels, you can put angel cards, or angel statues.

Raphael is in the East and represents the element of air; he is the archangel in charge of healing, science and knowledge. So I put things that represent these elements in the eastern section of my home, such as incense, feathers, wisdom books, healing tools.

Michael represents the South, truth, courage, protection and the element of fire. In this corner I have a candle representing transformation by fire, a miniature sword of truth and a small piece of blue material representing his cloak of protection.

Gabriel represents the West, the messenger angel, overseer of communication and the element of cleansing through water. So in the west I have a beautiful glass that I fill with natural water from a spring or river when I can, but tap water works just as well. Or you could use an indoor fountain. I put representations of what I try to communicate to people about spiritual development in this sector.

In the North stands Uriel, angel of the Earth who brings groundedness, determination and transmutes energy into action. So in the north I have crystals, a small bowl of earth, a stone from the garden, a plant. I also try to find something that represents the re-growth of life from death and the transformation cycle. This can be a piece of last year's dead wood with a new shoot on it or a picture of a butterfly. Butterflies are good because they hold the caterpillar, pupae, and butterfly signifying the various total transformations that can take place in a lifetime.

I also put things that have special meanings on my altar, such as Mothers' Day cards made for me by my children, and prayers or poems that mean a lot to me. It is a special place for special things. Because I am a healer I also keep photographs and my distant healing list in the east with Archangel Raphael.

In the bag I take around with me I have a crystal and talisman associated with each angel. For instance when doing readings my table is set up with the tape recorder and tapes in the west for Gabriel and communication, crystals in the north for Uriel and earth, a light or candle when possible in the south representing Michael, and my cards in the east, with feathers and incense representing healing and Raphael. So my table becomes an altar wherever I am and no-one else is aware but the angels and myself. My little secret with the angels.

You can have as much fun as you like creating and recreating your altar. They say angels fly because they take themselves lightly and as long as you are having fun with what you do then you are including them. It does not have to be too serious. My inner child is playing and that is what the angels like most and respond to. So ensure you are having fun in your own way.

How to ask the Angels for Help

The important thing is to ask the angels for help from an open and loving heart. To let go of the results and to really want them to bring you what's best for you and your loved ones for the highest good of all concerned.

Praying is often what's called asking. Whether you are praying to your own God / Goddess or to a particular angel makes no difference. It needs no particular words. The best way is just an imaginary conversation in your mind.

You can stand before your altar, (or because mine is by the side of my bed I lie down). At night I usually dump all my problems, fears, anxieties and ask them to let me know what I need to know most right now when I wake up and to give me a good night's sleep. When I wake up I say thank you, notice what comes to mind first and act accordingly, doing whatever I can and letting the rest go. I ask for the help I need. Sometimes I am not aware of what that might be so I ask in general terms to send me what I need to know for my highest good and the wisdom to notice it. I will often cut and angel card and see what it says. It is always the guidance I need.

Sometimes I have not known what I wanted or needed but I have felt deep in myself that something needs to shift. So I just sat and allowed myself to surrender to whatever is best for myself and all concerned. Within two days I felt better and on the third day things started to happen and change around me. The results were what I had wanted but not consciously been aware of.

For now all you have to do is ask. When asking for a specific angel remember that although it is useful to know the name of the angel you wish to ask for help, it is not essential. Remember that angels are energy, part of the all, and as long as you know the quality you wish to connect to that is sufficient. It is more important to focus on the quality of the energy you are connecting to. If you want courage, you could ask for the angel of courage to be with you, this would bring Archangel Michael to you. Try some of the suggestions below and notice what happens. Keep your notes in your journal for reference.

You don't need to just keep angelic help for serious or painful areas of your life. You can also ask for the angel of fun and laughter to be with you, for joy and happiness to enter your life. You don't need to be specific with things like "Make the person I have my eye on ask me out so I can be happy and go and have fun" because if that is not for the highest good of you both it won't happen and you'll stay miserable. Instead you can say "Please can the angel of fun and laughter enter my life today" and then watch how you start to notice funny things and share your delight with all sorts of people during the day, which makes you happier and more contented and puts more positive energy into your life thus getting more positive energy out into the universe to magnify and come back to you.

Don't forget the car parking angel. Some people ask for a parking space before going out. Personally I always forget and only ask when I get there. Know that you will get the space you need, where you need it, so don't get angry if the traffic stops, they may need to slow you down so you are in the right place at the right time.

You can make up angels because there are so many, supposedly one for everything. I remember when I worked in the City (before I gave up my day job and became a professional healer and teacher) I sent up a prayer to the angel of the underground for a seat, if no one needed it more than me, by the next station. I got a seat and from then on in I always got a seat either immediately I got on the train or by the next station. I just seemed to stand in front of whoever was getting off next. I had stood on the underground on the way home in rush hour for 25 years, and for the last couple of years I always had a seat. You have to remember to ask.

You can write to the angels as well. For instance, make a list of the qualities you want in your life, then burn it. Send it to the angels and ask them to bring it to you when the time is right and if it is for your highest good. You can be as specific as you like.

I once asked for a moon shadow blue, Peugeot 206 cabriolet, automatic (of which there are not many) at a price I could afford. At the time I could see no way of ever being able to afford one. Plus I had a car that worked so I did not need one.

About three months later on a Monday morning I received an unexpected cheque for £3,000. A friend suggested that I keep some of it because I might need a new car soon. That afternoon I did not get a parking space where I wanted one and I happened to park outside a Vauxhall garage which had my dream car right in front of me for £13,000. I walked in and put a deposit on it.

I had £3,000, and they were going to give me £1,000 on my old car and could offer me finance on the rest. I have never taken finance and did not want to take on a loan of this size when my income was so precarious. This is when I did not trust and things started to go wrong. I did not want to pay 15 per cent interest on the loan so thought I would apply for an increase in my mortgage. This was turned down so I assumed I was not meant to have the car and cancelled the transaction on the Friday and lost my deposit. Saturday morning at 06.00am my car broke down on the M25 motorway. I was stranded for three hours before I was towed off. My car was never to be seen again. The engine had seized completely. That afternoon I went into the garage, took the finance and bought the car. I had lost the £1,000 they had offered me on my car. An expensive lesson in trust.

To end the story, three months later my children came into an inheritance and gave me £10,000 to pay off my loan. The lesson is, if you have asked the angels to help you, trust what comes your way, however it comes, and expect the unexpected because all will be well in the end.

Beware of what you ask for because you might get it. If you are writing to the angels or making lists and asking for things, be careful you are sure you know what you want, for you might get it. I once wrote a list of all the qualities I wanted in my next partner. To name but some, he had to be spiritual, he had to dance, be wealthy, and good-looking. Three days later I met this paragon of virtue. He had everything on my list but I had omitted the qualities I did NOT want, such as controlling, arrogant, plus the obvious four letter word LOVE. He was definitely not what I wanted but I did get what I asked for. So be careful.

TRUST is the key element and be aware of what you learn so you can let go.

Angels also like it when you say thank you. The more you ask them to help and invite them into your life, the more you notice how your life becomes easier and runs more smoothly. You notice you are now more prepared to go with the flow and enjoy the unexpected. The more you notice the more you'll trust and the more you trust the more they will do and the happier you'll be. It really is that simple, **ask, notice, thank you.**

Getting the Answers

Angels use various ways of communicating with you. From signs like white feathers coming to you, signifying either you are about to receive something special so take extra notice of it, or "well done" you have just made a good decision.

They will use human people; they will bring someone into your life with a piece of information, which will make everything clear. They will send more than one person bringing you the same information, all mentioning the same book that might help you. You might find yourself drawn into a bookshop browsing for no reason and see the very book everyone has mentioned to you. It is still your choice whether you buy it or not, and then it is your choice whether you read it, but if you take notice of the signs you will start to notice how much more smoothly your life begins to flow.

Angels love music and use it as signs in many different ways. Song lines going through your head over and over but not going away until you connect them to your questions and what's going on in your life, can be a way of hearing an angelic message. If the song title or lyric doesn't answer your question then think back to what was going on in your life when the song first came out, identify the pattern, and you have the answer. You can also ask things such as "What is the meaning of an issue in my life?" or "What do I need to do about a certain situation?" then ask for the answer to be the third, fourth, fifth record from now on the radio. It's spookily accurate. As the radio alarm goes off in the morning the song on the radio answers questions you asked as you went to sleep. Don't ask me how it works, but it does.

Meditation is a way of listening to the answers from your angels. If you have never meditated don't worry it is not difficult – see suggested reading. By going deep into yourself, to the stillness, you connect to your own inner wisdom which is connected to the collective universal web of knowledge and you receive information directly either as a voice in your head or as a feeling in your body. If you are connected to your own feelings and trust your gut instincts and act on them you are following the guidance of your soul, and the angels and guides work that way too.

People often ask how to tell whether the information that comes into their heads during meditation is from angels and guides or from their imagination. Imagination is our umbilical cord to spirit. It is our creative link with the universal creative energy of which everything is a part. If you imagine something why do you imagine that particular thing at that particular moment which answers your question or someone else's needs. You need to learn to trust your imagination.

Another thing is that if you notice when you are imagining something or you're a getting your voice in your mind with an answer, the voice will be on the right side of your head. This is your right intuitive creative psychic brain that is the creative side and link to the universe (it controls the lefthand side of your body). The left-brain is your mind and person-ality, everything you have learned (and controls the righthand side of your body). If you feel a thought float in to the left of your head it is a thought, if it comes in to the right it is an answer. Noticing this takes practice but with practice it gets easier as you gain the inner confidence of knowing.

Trust as always is the key element.

Symbols and dreams

Angels often use symbols and dreams to send messages. Pictures speak a thousand words. This is not the place to discuss dream interpretation (see recommended reading) but I will give an example to illustrate it using my own experience.

The symbols given to you are for you and you need to interpret them. It is what they mean to you that is important, not what is written in a book. If you have never seen a shape or something before then of course researching and asking others is useful but at the end of the day it is what's in the answer that resonates with you that is important.

Take the Caduceus for instance. This is a symbol often used to represent healing and Archangel Raphael. It is two snakes entwined around a rod, coming together at the top with two wings. The snakes cross at all the chakra points from base to third eye. The rod can represent the body, the snakes activate the chakras, the third eye opens to cosmic knowledge, and the kundalini rises up the rod and out of the crown forming the wings of a free spirit.

In this symbol the wings have always been what I noticed so I need to interpret it according to what wings mean to me. Wanting to be a free spirit and noticing how much of my life I restrict. Snakes may be what someone else notices and for them it would need to be interpreted by what snakes mean to them. The rod may be what someone else focuses on. At different times in my life I may be drawn to other parts of the symbol, such as the snakes. What comes to me currently about snakes is that they shed their skin as they grow. Perhaps it is time for me to shed a skin, or a persona that I carry about who I am or what I am or am not capable of. Time to shed the skin and let the spirit fly again to a new level, a new chapter in my life.

Symbols have different meanings in different cultures and this is why you need to interpret what a symbol means to you. For instance in western cultures owls usually mean wisdom but in Native American culture they mean deception. So it is important to interpret symbols for yourself. In most books horses mean power but for me they are about freedom. See how I keep coming back to freedom, what is this telling me?

When you dream keep a dream diary. Angels will use dreams to communicate with you. If you write them down you'll begin to see a pattern forming which will point you in the direction you need to be taking or confirming that where you are and what you are currently doing is just right.

There are many different ways of interpreting dreams, we have discussed briefly how to interpret the symbols in a dream but there are also the dreams themselves.

Dreams work on many levels. They act as a way of the brain sorting relevant and irrelevant information. They act as a means of communication from your higher self and the angels through your unconscious to your conscious mind. Dreams often don't seem to relate to anything at all. Just a higgledy-piggledy mess, but when you stop and begin to play with a dream it can become quite easy to understand.

Because dreams are multi-levelled you can work with them on multi levels as well. One by taking each individual part of a dream as a symbol and asking yourself what the symbol might mean and the other by accepting that each element of a dream is representative of part of your personality. When you accept this you can work imaginatively with it.

I will illustrate what I mean with a personal example of a dream I had about eight years ago, four years after my husband's death.

As with all dreams it seemed very odd and jumbled to begin with. I was in the sitting room of my old house watching television with my children. The floor was cracked, with great big gaps, and the room seemed to be slipping away down the hill. In the middle of the room was a piece of machinery. It looked like a misshapen tree. A root seemed to be trying to hold a crack together, a branch seemed to trying to hold the ceiling up. As we watched television, huddled together in a corner, the tree kept sprouting new roots and branches, trying to keep everything together and protect us all. I noticed all this but did not seem bothered. In fact it all seemed quite normal to me.

I went into the kitchen to get something and noticed that at the back of the house the garden was being built on. There was a huge great, ugly glass building being constructed in my garden. It was completely overpowering my home. I returned to the sitting room and tried to ignore what was happening at the back. This state continued for a few weeks or months and the monstrosity at the back got bigger and bigger and more and more dangerous because nothing seemed to be holding it up, while in the sitting room the metal tree was continuing to sprout more and more branches and roots as the house continued to keep slipping and falling down around me.

Then, as happens in dreams, I seemed to be walking down railway tracks going through the middle of a desert. I felt as if I was going to work but I had missed the train. The children were not there but my dog was following me. My dog would not go home when he was told; he just trudged on behind me. He had a cut on his head and was bleeding. (In real life he had had a cut on his head which bled for a while, he had escaped from the garden as a puppy and had run across the road and been clipped by a passing car). I was following the tracks because that way I would not get lost and I hoped to catch up with the train. (Strange ideas we have in dreams). I was getting more and more angry with the dog because he would not do as he was told. I was really quite nasty to him but he just kept following me. Eventually I gave up telling him off and just let him come with me. I was comforted by his loyalty.

Then I woke up.

At first the two parts of this dream did not seem as if they went together. It felt like they were two different dreams. I started with the train track one because it seemed easier.

Trying to catch up with a train taking me to work made sense, I felt I had a long way to go with my career and that most people were succeeding quicker and better than me. (They were on the train). The desert also made sense. I felt, at that time, that I had no particular skills or experience, and no specific career or outcome in mind. I was just working to pay bills. My dog was the bit that interested me. So I used the following technique.

I relaxed, closed my eyes and went back into the dream in my imagination. First I took the role of my dog. I started to ask my dog questions. I had a conversation with myself in my imagination. It went something like this:

"What are you doing, what part of me are you, I have told you to go home and you just follow me, what's going on?"

He looked at me from those sad brown eyes and replied, "I am the part of you who loves you unconditionally. I am your love and your joy but you keep trying to put me behind you, but I am always there, following you, wherever you go."

This took me a bit by surprise. My love and my joy – but I thought I was happy. My dog did not look happy. Perhaps I was not as happy as I thought. Next I asked him about his head that was bleeding. For this there was no answer. "That you need to find for yourself," he said. So, adding another technique I decided to become the blood dripping from his head. I imagined myself being the blood coming from his head, and asked myself what I represented, what part of me was this blood? The answer was shocking. The blood responded that it was my pain. It would always be there, it could not be left behind, it could not be ignored, it could only be healed by accepting it as a fundamental part of myself.

Now it was making sense, my love, my joy, my pain, were all part of myself, all part of my life, I could not just cut off a part of myself and leave it at home. It went wherever I went. I could not be free of it. Dogs are very loyal, loving and never let us down. So here was a loyal loving part of myself that carried all my pain (of my mother's death when I was nine years old), which I was trying to ignore.

Next I started on the other part of the dream. My old house falling apart made sense because my life had fallen apart. My husband had died and I had created a new career for myself in marketing so that I could put the children through university. I was now a single parent, working a 60-hour week, at a job I thought I was very good at but most probably was not as good at as I thought. I certainly didn't like it as much as I had hoped and definitely didn't find it fulfilling. I had never had the time to grieve for my husband and my lost life and dreams. I was always too busy trying to survive.

I became the iron tree, which by now was very ugly and straining to keep the house together. What was I? I was the part of me that managed, that kept things together, that was very strong and never gave up. But I was very tired and would appreciate a break if possible. The house was falling down, I really was not sure I could keep it going any longer and I got to feel exactly how unhappy I really was. Why did I demand so much of myself? What could I do or change to relieve myself of this burden? Why could I not just give myself a break? What was I avoiding by doing all this? My pain and unhappiness, of course. Quite a realisation. I had what I thought I wanted: a good career, home, children, but I was unhappy. I needed to be doing something else. I noticed how unhappy and sad my children were, after all they hardly ever saw me and when they did I was tired and bad tempered. The tree went on for a very long time. Boy, did I give it to myself.

I then asked about the glass-house with no foundations out the back and was told it was my ego building a new career with no foundations. It was an ugly monstrosity that was not part of who I was, it was an illusion and if I allowed it to get any bigger it would destroy all of us. Heavy stuff. But I had to acknowledge the truth of it. I hardly ever saw my children, I was not happy in the new career, financially it was very rewarding but I found it frustrating and did not feel at home or comfortable in the business environment and never had. It had taken many years and a peculiar dream to admit that to myself.

So, metaphorically speaking, I left the old house and the new glass-house behind and moved out into the world to see what else there was and where I should go next.

Now the train in the desert took on new meaning. Perhaps I was not catching up, perhaps I was looking for something new. Perhaps I needed to accept the pain, rather than trying to run away from it. The dream was beginning to make sense. It was telling me to stop trying so hard to keep things the same and to explore the new. It was telling me I could not leave behind parts of myself behind that I did not want to acknowledge, I needed to accept them.

I arranged a holiday for myself and the children. I took the time to review my work and my skills, what I enjoyed and what I did not. Usually just before bed because I obviously still had to work and pay the bills whilst discovering what I might actually want. I started to notice the things in life that made me feel happy. The sun, the trees, my family and animals.

After my husband's death I had started to explore life, death, world religions and philosophies. I learned healing. I was already a Reiki Master doing healing and clairvoyance at weekends, but not as a full time career. I noticed it was when I was doing these things in my spare time, when I was helping people, that time flew by and I was happiest. At work what I enjoyed doing most was the staff personal development part of my job. So I decided to change my life again but this time in a gentler more caring manner for myself and my family. I started to slow down and stopped trying to catch up with the train. The desert was a quiet restful place for a while and when I slowed down enough the angels connected to me and showed me a new path out of the desert.

Remember this technique because later, as you journey to meet your spirit guides and angels, the symbolic journeys will yield a rich mosaic of how you and your unconscious view your life and what you need to do to create the life you want.

As you can see symbols and dreams are a complicated subject but it is what things mean to you that is most important. See the recommended reading list for more information on this.

Angel Cards

There are many different types of angel cards on the market that you can buy. You just need to allow yourself to be drawn in one way or another to whichever one you like. I use many different types. It could be the colour that draws you, or a word in the description. Just ask your angel to lead you to whichever you need for your highest good right now and trust your instincts. Whichever deck you buy will have instructions on their particular use.

Cards can be used in many different ways. You can ask a question and draw one or three cards. I usually draw one and trust whatever I get. Some people prefer to draw three cards: the first is the unconscious issue, the second what is stopping or what you need to do next, and the third is the outcome. Because angels work on your intention you can specify exactly what you want for any position. So you can ask many questions and get further clarification each time.

The simple way is to draw a card from your favourite deck and just ask for what you need to know or to focus on right now in your life. So for instance, one day I might draw the Angel of Boundaries. This tells me I am being guided not to let people impose on my space, to ensure I get time to myself; it is reminding me to say No. Later in the day, I may notice someone is asking me to fit in an extra appointment on my first day off in a couple of weeks. Their need seems to be great and I am about to give in when I remember the card I drew in the morning and I say No. I have held my boundaries. I need to recharge my batteries if I am to help others. They then make an appointment for the following week, which initially had been impossible for them. If instead I had drawn the Angel of Mercy I would have said Yes to the client, knowing that, in this case, it was necessary and trusting that somewhere, something else would get cancelled to give me a day off.

If you are feeling down, some angel cards have spiritually uplifting messages, which can make you see things differently and lift your spirits. I know one person who swears that what got her through breast cancer were the Angels of Light cards by Diana Cooper, because the messages always brought her hope, love and confidence in her future.

Alternatively you can make your own cards. Using card, paper, crayons, paint, shapes, whatever you feel is right for you. Simple words, spiritual messages, whatever you are guided to do. Simply connect to your guardian angel and create whatever comes to you. You will be guided.

CHAPTER 3

Chakras and Auras

The Body's Energy System

Before we proceed, you'll need to know a little about the bodies energy system and how to open and close your chakras. There is so much written on chakras so if you want to go into more depth then see the recommended reading list but I like to keep things simple and this is all you actually need to know.

What Are The 7 Major Chakras?

Everything has an aura, energy field around it, which can be photographed using special cameras. Our aura holds all the information both positive and negative from our past, present and future lives which is why healing in the aura is so powerful.

We need to understand the chakra system because it has a direct connection to our physical, emotional and spiritual well-being. Understanding its functions can help us respond to life with awareness rather than being unconsciously reactive. Emotional and past life traumas are stored in the chakras and by clearing them we can help ourselves move forward in our lives.

The word chakra itself is Sanskrit (ancient Hindi) and means "wheel". When you see the chakras, which you can with special cameras, they are like spinning energy vortices, and are funnel-shaped. The wider, spinning end interacts with our auric field, whilst the stem appears to be embedded in our spine. The vortices go in both directions through the front and back of the body with the centre of the funnel joining in the centre channel, which runs through the centre of our body.

Chakras act as step-down transformers, converting subtle energy – prana, chi, Reiki, universal cosmic energy, (for me this is God's love), to be used by the hormonal, nervous and cellular systems of our physical body. We take in air and food to fuel the molecular building blocks of our body. The aura and chakras take in the subtle energy, which is also fundamental for life. As well as being linked to the physical functioning of our bodies each chakra holds a key to understanding our relationships, our strengths and weaknesses and our sense of who and what we are in the world.

The 7 major chakras each have
Different frequencies
Different colours associated with them
Relationships with different emotional and spiritual issues
Connections to different endocrine gland and nerve plexus
Different governing elements (earth, water, fire, air, ether)
Different gemstones, aromas, and angels to help balance them.

There are many other minor chakras (189 some specialists say), in the palms of the hands, soles of the feet, behind the knees, in the crook of the elbows and scattered throughout the body at strategic positions relevant to the energetic functioning of our physical and etheric bodies. These are all the points along the meridians used by complementary therapies aimed at clearing blockages in the body such as shiatsu and acupuncture.

It is important for all the chakras to be energised and functioning efficiently for the all round well being of the individual on all levels, physical, emotional, spiritual.

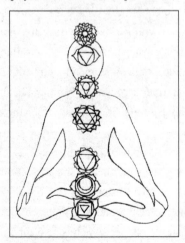

We are third dimensional beings and the colours shown are those recognised in the ancient Indian yogic tradition as well as in new age healing circles. As we progress on our spiritual journey then our body's vibrations are raised. We become more aware and as this happens then the colours in our chakras change. If you see other colours than those I mention then stay with what you have. We are all different and they are constantly

7 LAYERS OF THE AURA

- The universal energy field connects to the human energy field (aura).
- The aura consists of 7 main layers (see diagram).
- These layers encompass our physical body and are seen as oval shaped, starting from the first layer which is approximately ¼ - ½ inch from the physical body ranging to the seventh layer which is approximately 4 ft. away from the physical body.

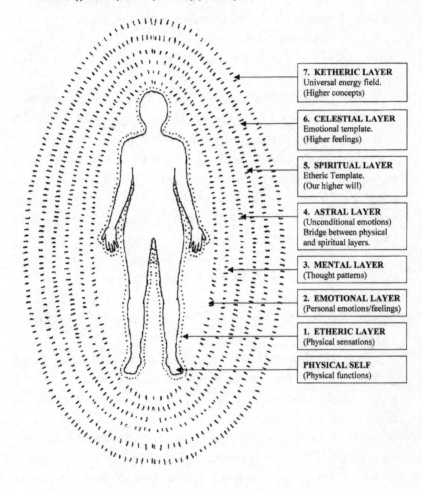

7. KETHERIC LAYER
Universal energy field.
(Higher concepts)

6. CELESTIAL LAYER
Emotional template.
(Higher feelings)

5. SPIRITUAL LAYER
Etheric Template.
(Our higher will)

4. ASTRAL LAYER
(Unconditional emotions)
Bridge between physical
and spiritual layers.

3. MENTAL LAYER
(Thought patterns)

2. EMOTIONAL LAYER
(Personal emotions/feelings)

1. ETHERIC LAYER
(Physical sensations)

PHYSICAL SELF
(Physical functions)

changing.

The energy from these chakras form our aura, which is the energy surrounding us. Through our chakras, our meridian system and the aura we connect to the energy of mother earth, through her ley lines, and the universal matrix of energy of all there is.

Hints and tips to connect quickly

As you progress you'll find the more you do the exercises the quicker you get at it. But there are some shortcuts you can use as well. In NLP (Neuro Linguistic Programming – see further reading), these are called anchors. In the next exercise I will talk of the red 3, green 2 and white 1, these are anchors. Anchors are something you associate with a particular memory or state, a combination of feelings, senses and emotions, such as feeling confident.

Anything can be used as an anchor. Breath, touch, smell, sound, colour, or a combination, it's really up to you. The suggestions that follow are things I have found, over the years, work for most people. The objective is to associate something with a particular state you wish to reconnect to. For instance the smell of cloves for me reminds me of sweets, winter evenings, Christmas. For others it is associated with toothache. The words of a song may take me back to a good or bad time in my life, where I re-experience those feelings.

At various points as you do the meditations we will add some anchors to enable you to go directly back to that space in future meditations. We will also be creating anchors, at different times, by pressing our thumb and different fingers tightly together to allow you to return to that particular part of the journey.

As you go through the exercises, focus on exactly how you feel in your body at specific times; how your really feel. I have put in quite a few different steps but as you get proficient you'll be able to leave them out and go straight to wherever you want to be.

Burning different incenses for each angel is helpful because smell is a very powerful anchor. But keep to the same one for each, such as lavender for your guardian angel, sandalwood for Raphael, myrrh for Michael or whatever you choose. These incenses will enable you to quickly reconnect to your experiences in the future. As soon as you smell a particular smell you can re-associate yourself with the experience.

Please remember the meditative journeys I take you on are just suggestions. Following your own journey in your own imagination is what's most important. Whatever you imagine, wherever you end up, is exactly right for you. If I say something is one colour and you get another, it just means that you may need something different at this time, it does not mean you are doing it wrong. Trust that what you get is what you need. The angels know what's right for you.

Now we will do a visualisation to open and close your chakras and introduce you to another method of protecting yourself. The more you do this the quicker it will become. As you progress, the shape of your protection, which will be whatever you need it to be for you, will change with the work you do. Just notice what it is for you and if you don't see or sense anything then imagine it being whatever you'd like it to be. For instance, mine was always a golden pyramid that I see through and which goes under my feet and over my head. Over the years it has changed through various stages, including a merkaba (a sacred geometric shape) and is now much more complex. Some people have an egg shape, or pyramid shape, often in gold or silver. Whatever it is, just know it's right for you and that only positive energy can pass through it and any negative energy will be transmuted and turned into pure, positive, loving energy and sent back where it came from.

Later we will go up through the dimensions to the 4th dimension where spirit guides and loved ones reside, and the 5th dimension, where the angels reside. At each stage we will bring down the appropriate colours for each chakra, but please remember, (and I cannot emphasise this enough), whatever you get is just right for you.

We will also be pressing our fingers and thumbs together at significant stages such as the 4th dimension when you have met your spirit guide and the 5th dimension when you have met your guardian angel. This will allow you to return to these places immediately in the future with practice. For reference these are the fingers we will be using are :

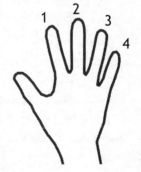

Some people see the chakras as flowers with the petals opening and closing, or clear quartz crystals which take on colour. Others as little doors of different colours. Even as spinning vortexes. However you see your chakras is just right for you.

Chakra Opening *(This will be on a CD)*

"Now, if you would like to close your eyes and relax; make yourself comfortable and start to focus on your breathing. Focus on your breathing, breathing very gently in and out, in and out; say to yourself, "I am breathing in peace and love and breathing out all negativity, breathing in peace and love and breathing out all negativity." Breathing in peace and love and with each out-breath you become more and more relaxed. Leaving all problems and worries, leaving them all behind you, just breathing them all away, breathing them out, and as you breath out you become more and more relaxed, more and more relaxed, going deeper and deeper into relaxation; becoming more and more relaxed. Your body is feeling heavy and relaxed as you sink deeper and deeper into relaxation. Breathing in peace and love and going deeper and deeper into your body. That's right. Good.

So feel your feet on the ground and imagine your feet having roots; imagine those roots going deep into the ground, pushing down deep into the ground, taking any negativity with them, with each out breath pushing those roots deep into the ground.

Now focus on the base of your spine. With each out-breath imagine the base of your spine getting longer and longer, pushing down deep into the earth, deep down amongst the rocks, pushing down and wrapping around something very solid so you are truly connected to Mother Earth.

Now focus on your in-breath and breathe up the earth energy; up through your roots, up through the elongated spine. Feel that energy coming up, up and into your feet.

Feel your feet relax and as your feet relax and become warm, notice that warm healing earth energy coming up through your feet, up into your calves, feeling warm and light and heavy. As you breathe in, breathe the energy up through your knees and up into your thighs, feel those thigh muscles relax; feel them relax, warm and heavy, letting go of all tension.

And as you breathe in, feel the energy come up into the base chakra and feel the base chakra open turning a brilliant shade of red, and see a big red 3 in front of you. Feel that energy spreading around your base, filling your bones, warming and relaxing.

Now breathe the energy up into the sacrum, just below the navel; feel that sacrum chakra turning a beautiful shade of orange, brilliant orange and feel that chakra spread that orange all the way around, round your hips, round the lower tummy, relaxing and warming. And as you breathe the energy up into the solar plexus, feel the solar plexus open and start to turn a brilliant shade of yellow, warm and happy, feel that energy spread around your midriff round your back, relaxing taking you to new levels of relaxation.

And as you draw that energy up, up into the heart chakra, feel the heart chakra open, feel your heart open, feel the unconditional love in your heart pouring out into your aura, into the world, and see a big green 2 in front of you. Feel the energy relaxing and warming through your chest, both front and back.

And as you breathe in again breathe in the energy up to the throat. Feel the throat chakra open turning a brilliant shade of blue; feeling the throat chakra open.

As you begin to draw the energy up into your face up towards the third eye, feel all the muscles in your face relax, those little muscles round the mouth, nose and the eyes relaxing; and your jaw relaxes as you draw the energy to the third eye and you feel the third eye open, turning purple.

And as you draw the energy to the crown feel the energy at the top of your head tingle and know the energy is coming out of the top of your head tumbling around you, cleansing your aura.

And as you draw this energy together you are feeling deeply relaxed, very safe, very secure and you see a big white 1 going up out of your head up into the sky to join with the silver golden energy of the universe which you breathe in, down through your crown, down through your body and you are drawing down the pure universal healing energy. Filling your body and your aura with love. The energy passes straight through you and down through your feet to replenish the energy of Mother Earth.

See that energy coming out of your crown, filling your aura and forming a hard transparent shell all around you. Notice what shape or colour this shell is. Know that only unconditional love can penetrate this shell. Anything of a lower vibration will be transformed into unconditional love and sent back to wherever it came from. You are truly protected from both deliberate and accidental negative energies affecting you or your life. This shell is so impenetrable that nothing that is not for your highest good can pass through including germs, infections, viruses and allergies.

Now press your thumb and first finger together really tightly. Just sit in this space for a few moments enjoying the energy, that's right just feel the energy for a few moments.

(If you are taping this pause for a couple of minutes before progressing)

Now letting go of your thumb and first finger focus on your breathing again and start to see the white light come down through your body and fill you with healing energy as you feel the light push the colours down through your third eye; and see the third eye close and the purple fade away.

As the white light continues down, you see and feel the heart close as the green and pink fade away and you see and feel the solar plexus close and the yellow fade away, the sacrum closes and the orange fades away and as the base closes, the red fades away. Now you see yourself as a pillar of white light connecting the universe to Mother Earth.

Now focus on your in-breath; breathe up the roots from the earth back into your feet and close the foot chakras and pull up your elongated spine and curl it back into the base of your spine.

Lastly cut the cord of silver white light above your head and let the universal energy drift away as you close your crown chakra. Know that you are fully closed and protected and ready to return to the present fully refreshed and energised and ready to go about your business. Knowing that you can do this again at any time just by focusing on your breathing and breathing your roots into the ground, breathing the energy up to the base chakra and seeing the big red 3, breathing in again up to the heart chakra and the big green 2 and breathing up to the crown and the big white 1 to open and see the energy forming and recharging the protection around you.

Then seeing the colours disappear as you breath out down to the heart and see the heart chakra close as the green 2 disappears, breathing down to the base and breathing up your roots into your base as the big red 3 disappears; then closing the crown and watching the white light and the big white 1 disappears.

So slowly come back into the present. Feel your fingers and feet start to move and gently open your eyes. You may like to have a glass of water now just to bring you back to the present.

Well done.

This is an important exercise because we shall be using it to start and end all other exercises so please practice it. Each time you practice it it will get quicker and quicker until you can open up with just the three breaths. Eventually you'll be able to do it in one breath out and in and pressing your thumb and index finger together.

If you can get in the habit of opening before you do any spiritual work and closing at the end you'll soon become very proficient and fast at this exercise.

Also remember that ensuring you are closed before travelling on public transport will stop anyone leeching energy from you. I am sure many of you have been on public transport going somewhere and when you arrive you can't imagine how sitting on a train or a bus could have made you feel so tired. Make sure you keep your chakras closed and breathe your aura into just a few inches from your body and you'll never feel so tired again, nor will you get that feeling of being crowded. Enjoy practicing.

Now you have learned to connect and protect yourself with universal energy we will begin to look briefly and simply at how this energy can be used for your own healing and personal development and that of others and the planet before we start to go through the dimensions to meet your spirit guide and the angels.

CHAPTER 4

Healing

What is Universal Healing Energy?

There are so many different types of energy healing, Reiki, Spiritual
Healing, Reconnective Healing, Quantum Touch, Tera Mai, Seichem, to
name but a few with more coming daily. Although they all purport to be
different, I believe they are essentially the same. Whatever you call it and
however you do it, you are connecting to the same source of energy. The
methods vary, the vibrations vary, but the energy you connect to is the
same. The difference is in the frequency of the energy the healer can
channel and the healee can receive and this constantly changes as you do
more and more.

I believe, it's also affected by how much self-healing the healer has
done—the amount of their own issues and ego they have been able to let
go of. Everything you do within this book and in other areas of your life,
and the energy constantly raising on the planet with more and more people
becoming interested, then so the vibrations will continue to rise.

What is the Purpose of Healing?

Healing is about restoring the body's natural spiritual, mental, emotional
and physical balance, not curing. The aim is to heal holistically rather than
to treat any specific disorders. If the soul is ill-at-ease at any level, the
body reflects this dis-ease. The body has its own cellular memory, it knows
how it's supposed to be, so by connecting to universal life force energy
these different levels can be brought back into balance and the body
restores itself.

To do this the healer connects to the universal life force energy of
unconditional love with Archangel Raphael. By learning healing you can
start your own journey of spiritual and personal development as well as
learning how to help others.

What is healing?

To heal you need to let go of trying to get any particular result. It is not easy to let go of the result because we all think we know what is best for us and our loved ones and there will always be a human part of us that wants recognition.

Be aware that healing is not curing. Healing energy is universal energy. It is the energy of unconditional love. When healing you are acting as a channel and the healing energy is being channelled through you from God/Goddess, Universal Creator (call this energy what you will) via the angels and your higher self to your soul, if you are doing self healing, or to the soul of another, if you are healing others, or even mother earth. This energy is passed unconditionally for the soul to use for its own highest good. We don't necessarily know what that is. We may think we do but we do not "know" what our soul wants. For instance, a soul may have chosen to experience death by cancer in this lifetime. It is not up to us as healer, or even their own conscious mind, to choose to deny this experience, although I have heard of some people who have re-written their soul contract whilst here.

What we can do is channel healing energy to the soul for their soul to use for their highest good. This may be to let go of fear, to speak and say what they need to say to their nearest and dearest. Of course, it may also be to help them let go of whatever deeply buried issues have been "eating away at them" so the body can heal itself and they can go on to live the life they came here to live.

There is much written about healing (some books are recommended at the end) and there are many different names and forms of healing. Suffice it to say that Archangel Raphael watches over all forms of healing from shamanistic methods and traditional herbalism, to modern phamaceutical medicine and all forms of energy healing in between, including crystals, colour therapy, Reiki, vortex, pranic, reconnective, and many more.

I believe all these methods to be equally valid; they are just different ways of connecting to the same energy and they all work on the power of your intention. If you are intending to channel loving energy for someone's highest good then that is what will happen. By letting go of what the energy is used for you ensure that it's used in a positive way. The only variation in all the above methods is the procedure and method itself which are all created in some way or other by different people. They all work but sometimes the more you know, the more you try and the less happens. At the end of the day keep it simple. The simplest way, and what I have found produces the best results, is simply to:

1. Open your chakras
2. Hold your hands out in front of you
3. Ask to connect to healing energy
4. Imagine and feel the energy coming down through your crown and out of your hands (this usually makes your hands warm and tingly, though for some it feels cold)
5. Ask that the energy be used for the highest good of the person you are giving it to, either yourself, or whomever, whether they are in your presence or not, just by saying their name
6. Place your hands either on the body or in the aura, if they are not present then imagine them with you, and channel the energy until you feel drawn to move on to another spot. You'll be drawn to wherever the energy needs to go and the energy will go to wherever it is needed. Just resting your hand on someone and connecting to the energy will allow that person to draw healing energy through you if they need it. If someone is not present (ie distant healing), just imagine them between your two hands and send the healing to them.

You can send healing energy to any part of the world or the planet itself. I usually just hold a ball in my hand and my intention is to send healing energy to mother earth to replenish her from everything humans have done and are still doing to her. This is a really lovely experience because you are then connected directly to the universe and to the planet and you can really connect to the vastness of everything and your own part in it.

Be aware that as you give a healing so you receive healing because the energy is coming through you. The more you heal yourself the clearer your channel will be to pass healing on. With each healing your vibrations will raise. Sometimes you will feel the energy and the tingling, sometimes you won't. This does not mean nothing is happening or that it's not working. It means that the energy vibration you are channelling is exactly the same as the vibration in your body therefore you can't feel the difference. Just keep healing and you will start to bring down a higher vibration and you will feel the energy again until your body raises its vibrations to the same level. Then it feels like it has gone again and the whole process starts over. Just keep at it.

I hope you enjoy this simple form of channelling healing energy because in my experience it brings about gentle positive changes in your life and can have far reaching results beyond anything you could imagine. I connect many people this way every year at the short workshops and demonstrations I do.

What you need to be aware of is that as the energy starts cleansing and detoxing your life, you may initially develop signs similar to cold symptoms as things held in your body are flushed out of your system. You may feel emotions and have memories that you have not experienced for some time. Just be aware that you are letting things go. Nothing can come up that you can't cope with because everything is being done angelically for your highest good. This is why it takes time.

Angel of Healing

Archangel Raphael is the archangel of healing, science and knowledge as well as ruler of the sun, ruling angel of Sunday and one of the four mighty archangels protecting the universe. He governs the east, the element of air. He is a ruling prince of the cherubim, as well as being a throne. Archangel Raphael and his angels are everywhere and anywhere at all times, overseeing everything to do with healing. That includes all forms of energy healing, the orthodox medical profession and research, as well as care workers, counsellors, psychotherapists and everyone when they are helping themselves and others. You can connect to Archangel Raphael to send healing energy to others who you feel may need it. Raphael connects with you when you connect to healing energy anyway but if you consciously connect to him first then the energy you channel seems stronger and more powerful.

Some people say you should never send healing to anyone unless they ask for it first but I feel that if you intend "to send the healing for someone's highest good and if they don't wish for it to send it on to someone who does or to mother earth herself" and your intention is that the healing energy is used for whatever purpose the receiver needs it (rather than whatever you might like to be trying to heal) then it is OK.

Healing energy is everywhere and you are already connected to it. The following exercise is a simple one to ask Archangel Raphael to assist in healing. This is being done at the third dimension but in later meditations you'll go up into the fourth dimension to meet your spirit guide and loved ones and also to the fifth dimension to meet your guardian angel and the rest of the angels. As you raise your vibrations with time and practice so you'll feel the energy get stronger.

Connecting to Archangel Raphael's Healing Energy

Allow yourself 20 - 30 minutes to do the exercise. Turn off the phone. Get yourself into a comfortable position.

To connect to any angel or archangel you must first open, ground and protect yourself. Use whichever quick way you are comfortable with right now. If you feel happy with using the more advanced anchor of pressing your thumb and index finger together then do so but I will be guiding you at this stage again with breathing down your roots and using the 3 2 1 anchors and reinforcing it with pressing your thumb and first finger together.

Remember you can anchor Raphael's energy either with a feeling, a smell, a colour or whatever suits you. When I first connected to Raphael I experienced a bright emerald green image and a tingling in my hands so when I want to reconnect to him I just ask for him in my mind – I set my intention: "I wish to connect to Archangel Raphael" and I wait until I can see myself surrounded by emerald green or gold energy and I feel my hands begin to tingle then I know the healing energy is with me. It may be different for you so notice things you can use for your own anchors. Remember that for the future you can give yourself an anchor for connecting to any angel.

Focus on your breathing then take a big in-breath and as you breathe out imagine your roots going deep into the ground. As you breathe in again imagine the energy coming up to your base chakra as you see a big red 3 in your base. Relax breathe out and as you breathe in again imagine the energy rising through your sacrum and solar plexus to your heart where you see the big green 2. Relax, breathe out and as you breathe in you feel the energy rise from your heart through and opening your throat, brow and crown, Feel the energy flow around you, cleansing your aura and forming the big white 1 above your head, joining with universal energy and coming down into your head, down to your heart and out into your aura strengthening your protection, as you press your thumb and first finger together you feel fully open and protected.

Now set your intention in your mind and your heart that you intend to invoke Archangel Raphael, angel of healing

Invoke Archangel Raphael by speaking his name three times in whichever way you wish. In your mind, heart or out loud. I usually say:

"Archangel Raphael, angel of healing, Raphael angel of the east, Raphael angel of the element of air, please be with me now to send healing to (say someone's name or a list of names) for their highest good and entirety."

Notice the energy coming through you and become aware of something you can associate with this particular angel energy again in the future.

Speak to Raphael, ask him what you need to do right now, what you may need to know, what areas in your life need attention. What is most important to you, how much time do you spend doing the things that are most important to you. What stops you? Listen to your imagination. Sense, see, feel, hear, whatever information is passed to you now. Remember. Notice how familiar the energy may be. You are probably re-awakening your own natural healing energies. Anchor this state in some way so you can return quickly to this energy. Perhaps with a colour or a smell.

When you have received all the information you can, or you feel the energy lessen, then say thank you and goodbye to Raphael, knowing you can return at any time in the future and that he will always be at your side when you ask.

Begin to focus on your breathing and letting go of any anchor you may have noticed, such as a colour or smell, just let it go and then let go of your thumb and first finger. Focus on your breathing, breathing up your roots with a big in-breath, seeing the red 3 fade away as the base chakra closes, breathing out the energy as you close the sacrum, solar plexus and heart as the big green 2 fades away. Feel the energy strengthening your protection before you cut the silver thread of universal energy as the big white 1 fades away. Gently return to the present by gently wiggling your fingers and toes and opening your eyes.

Have a glass of water and write down your experience in your journal, or draw a picture, whatever you need to allow yourself to ground the experience in your present.

Spirit Guides

There is so much written on spirit guides, a lot of which is contradicting, but as with my philosophy of keeping things simple, I shall keep this brief and just give you the information you need. If you want more information then please see the recommended reading list.

Spirit guides are human (or they were during their lifetime) and reside with your loved ones at the fourth dimension. They are very wise beings who have had many lifetimes. Part of their evolutionary journey is to assist souls on their human journey. They are with us from birth so they have to have passed over before we are born. They can be family members but usually are not. Your family and loved ones, who have passed, can come and give you messages but they are rarely your spirit guide.

You have one main guide with you from birth to death; and a variety of guides will come into your life at different times to help you with different areas of your life. You might find yourself drawn to different interests, such as crystals, healing, sharmanism, or parts of the world or Egyptian, Mayan, Tibetan cultures. This is when different guides come in to help you. All these interests and learning will come together, in time, so you have all the tools you need to complete your life's purpose.

When we travel to the fifth dimension to reach the angelic realms, we pass through the fourth dimension, where guides and relatives reside and here you can stop off and meet your spirit guide and your loved ones who may have passed. This is a very moving experience. All the exercises in this book are moving experiences and you need to be aware that anything that comes up for you is just right for you right now. Your own higher self, your spirit guides and guardian angels will not allow anything you can't cope with right now to present itself to you. This is why it is a continuing journey.

Our journey will be to meet your door-keeper, your main spirit guide, but we will be going to a special island via way of the dolphins. The most important part of this meditation is the journey itself. Notice whatever you can about the journey and if you want to stop the CD or come out of the meditation at any time to capture your experiences in your journal then do so.

The journey itself will give you so much information about how you view your life, its obstacles, how you overcome them and how your unconscious mind and emotions sees your world. This is very valuable because it starts the process of awakening your inner self so you can see where you are now and so start the journey back to wholeness and connect to those parts of yourself that you have been protecting, maybe behind layers and layers of defences as spoken of by Ithuriel at the beginning of this book.

I often see the process of life's journey as peeling the onion of my life. Taking off layer after layer of knowledge, inspiration, acceptance and understanding, to find the truth of myself and my own inner wisdom. This has had, and continues to have, the effect of improving all my interpersonal relationships and bringing more meaning, happiness and fulfilment to my life and I hope of those that come in contact with me.

Each layer of my onion has tears I need to shed, this may not be the case with you, you might have joy you have suppressed, and this is important because if the tears are not shed the grief enzymes contained in tears can eat away at you or turn to crystals in the blood and adhere themselves to the joints and can cause cancer or arthritis in later life. Plus under the tears and pain is the joy and happiness waiting to be set free. It is important to let those old emotions go even if you don't know what they are about so you can find your way to the centre of the onion which reveals the flower of your life and all that it holds.

Things to Remember before Meditative Journey Work

The worst thing you can do is not use your imagination and try too hard. The spirit and angelic realms use your imagination to communicate with you. It is your creative link with spirit. We are all divine beings who have chosen to inhabit a human body so we can experience ourselves. This is why the soul resides in the body not in the mind and the soul experiences itself through physical feelings, sensations, emotions. Most of us cut ourselves off from our feelings and try to do everything through our minds.

I think our mind is like a blank computer hard drive. From the time of its birth it stores all the information it receives and our mind tries to makes sense of everything it experiences. Its reference points are its past experience. Hence it can be misleading. We have all seen car number plates where our minds try and make sense out of random letters. We have all read them incorrectly to get them to make sense. We all have this personal evidence yet we still trust our mind rather than our body to make decisions.

We all know how wrong computers can be, how, if the software corrupts things can get lost and not be found. They need defragging to get them to sort out things that have been misfiled so they can become more efficient. So it is with your mind and in a way this is what we are doing with this book, defragging our minds. Using new tools and techniques to see if we can locate any misinformation, beliefs and patterns of behaviour that no longer serve us or that were misinformed to start with, letting them go and replacing them with new and more useful connections and experiences. Choosing and creating our own lives consciously with all our current knowledge rather than unconsciously with misinformation.

How To Interpret Your Journeys

Journey work is a very interesting phenomenon because it seems that whatever comes out of your imagination is very meaningful in so many ways. We will be doing a number of imaginative exercises in our journey to the angels and self-enlightenment and they will all open new areas of your unconscious for you to discover.

The first thing is to go into the exercise with an expectation of getting what you need, knowing that whatever you receive is what you need right now. Know that you can't do anything wrong. Know that all you need to do is relax and enjoy whatever comes and if nothing comes, use your imagination actively.

Remember *everything* on the journey will have some significance.

I am going to use an example from my own experience to describe how you can interpret your experiences on your journeys and get the most out of these exercises. The following is my first journey to meet my spirit guide.

My journey started in a meadow, a beautiful place in nature. I waited for something to appear and when nothing did, I started to remember beautiful places I had been in the past. Lots of lovely places went through my mind and I couldn't make up my mind where I wanted to be. I kept flitting from one memory to another. But I could hear a variety of birds, smell flowers, sense all the places and memories that I went to. I had just about settled on a childhood memory that seemed to be lots of places all mixed up when it was time to leave the meadow.

We were supposed to see a path going down a hill but mine went up, so after trying to make it go down a few times, I gave up and followed it up. It was quite a wide path to start with, then it narrowed, then it went through woods, it seemed to take on whatever words the facilitator said but still went up rather than down. There were quite a lot of obstacles in the way and it was interesting to see how I overcame them. Sometimes I climbed straight over the top, sometimes I went round, once I even tunnelled underneath, once I went back and took another path and rejoined the path later on. Some obstacles were fallen trees, some were big boulders, some were streams, one was a river I swam across, one was a big wall blocking the way. I was often tempted to go down other paths just to see where they led and I often did go down just a little way and then cut back across to the main path.

The path went up and up and went through lots of different types of vegetation. So from the meadow we went through fields then up into forest which started as mostly deciduous forests then became more pine trees as we went higher and higher until I got above the tree line and into grass and moor land, then up into rocks and mountains. Some of the places seemed familiar and were memories of places I had been that would fit with this very logical progression of going up a mountain. For me, although it was an imaginative journey, it also had to be logical. Sometimes the road was wide and easy to follow; sometimes it was very rugged and difficult.

Eventually I came round a corner and saw the most fantastic view of my life. I was looking down on snow-covered mountains. I felt free and on top of the world. The view was, in fact, something I had seen before one Easter in Switzerland when I was about seven or eight years old and I have never been able to find the place again. I looked around and was spell-bound by the view but I could not see my guide. I could sense an energy though.

I spent some time sensing the energy and asking myself what type of person would feel like this. I felt a very caring loving energy, which did touch me, and I felt very tearful. (But big girls don't cry). I followed the facilitators' instructions and had a conversation with my guide, I could feel them but had no image or voice just my own voice, asking questions, and imagining the answers. The answers were strange, though, because it was not using my usual terms of expression, although it sounded like me it made a lot more sense and seemed very caring, which again made me realise how little care or love I seemed to have experienced in my life.

When he told me he was pleased to meet me at last and that one day I was going to be a spiritual teacher and write books, I felt I was crazy talking such nonsense to myself. After all I failed English O Level so how could I write a book? He also said for now I needed to get to know and love myself. I was to notice my good qualities, notice my journey and give credit to myself. He said in this process I would learn how to help many other people. I was definitely crazy! After all I was developing my career as a strategic marketing director and intended to have my own business. Anyway I played along and asked how I should get to know myself. He said I needed to do a counselling course. Nothing was further from my mind at that time.

Then I thought to myself that I actually wanted to have a person I could connect to, a name and a face. Someone I could turn to. I liked the feel of the energy I was with but I wanted more, as usual. So I asked if I could give him a name and a face because it would make it easier for me to communicate with him rather than just "OY! You up there". So I started to imagine what this energy might look like. A picture of Alec Guiness as Obe One Canobie in Star Wars appeared in my mind. All white, and long white robe. But his name was not Alec or Obe One, the name he gave me was Sebastian. So I created my guide myself.

I went back to my wonderful view regularly to talk to him and ask advice about what I needed to do next. I used to argue quite a lot a first but over time I began to realise that when I did at least investigate some of his suggestions I felt happier and more contented and things seemed to get easier rather than more difficult. He was right that first day, I did do a counselling training eventually and I did start to appreciate myself and my life more. Now I am a spiritual teacher, writing a book. But how did I get here from that original journey?

I drew the journey the beautiful meadow in the country of my childhood, the width of the paths, the different types of terrain and obstacles. How I got round those obstacles right the way up to the top of the mountain. This did not take long and I am not an artist, it was literally just matchstick men and child art. Then I sat back and thought about my life. The meadow of childhood, me happy before my mother died. The first change from the meadow to a very big lonely space before it became a small non-existent path that went straight into a big forest. So I followed my journey and related it all back to significant events in my life. If I was not sure then I used the dream interpretation technique of becoming the obstacle and asking what it was all about. The use of metaphor and imagination for interpretation just makes everything so much easier to see from a different perspective.

This is not a book about the story of my life but that first journey really opened my eyes to some of my qualities. My curiosity, wanting to go down other pathways just to see where they lead, my tenacity, I never gave up and always found a way round every obstacle, whatever it was and however big. My courage, drive and determination. My aloneness, I would never let anyone help me. The number of times I went off the path because another one looked easier but always ended up in a dead end and having to retrace my steps and usually getting lost for a while. After all, my life had not been easy, no one's is, but it had given me all those good qualities and I was grateful. In the eyes of the world I may be a complete nobody. No partner, no respected career, no money, few skills, just an ordinary person. But I did have all the qualities above, and two children and two dogs who loved me to bits. Now I could stop seeing myself as a victim whose mum had died when she was nine and who had never been good enough anyway, and start to notice that perhaps I was not all bad after all. All because I drew my journey and looked at it objectively through the eyes of my guide, and saw things as learning not failures.

I never really expected to do any of the things Sebastian told me I would at that time but I did make a start by looking more kindly on myself and investigating counselling training. Life moves on and when I do a journey now and check my path it is not going quite as steeply up hill. I now no longer have to take the most difficult way, I can meander slowly and enjoy the views.

I hope this example helps you to interpret and understand your own journeys.

Other things to note on your journeys are the types of houses, and dwellings that you create for yourself. These tell you a lot about yourself and how your unconscious sees yourself. Again what these images mean to you is what's important.

Five years after that first journey a Psychic Artist drew me a picture of my guide. He looked like Alec Guiness and his name was Sebastian. So what did I make up? Why did that particular image come to me when I wanted to see and connect? Trust your imagination.

Journey to Meet your Spirit Guide

Spirit Guides and loved ones reside in the fourth dimension so we are going to need to raise our vibrations to the fourth dimensional level when we journey there. Later when we journey to the angelic realms we will raise it again to the fifth dimensional level, but for now we will focus on the fourth.

One way of doing this, which I have found to be the quickest and most powerful, is to raise the frequency of the body's energy by bringing down the fourth dimensional chakras into your body. This is done imaginatively in the meditation we shall be doing soon. The other dimensional chakras do exist and there are aura photos to prove it but what's important to remember is that everyone is different. Various people have worked with the fourth dimensional chakras and most see them all slightly differently. Whatever you see or sense for yourself is just right for you right now. If you see different colours to those I set out below don't worry. It is your images and senses that are right for you. Over time they may change, mine have.

Table 1

Chakra	Third Dimension colour	Fourth Dimension colour (pastels)
Base	Red	Magenta
Sacrum	Orange	Peach
Solar plexus	Yellow	Primrose
Heart	Green / Magenta	Pastel Pink
Throat	Blue / Turquoise	Pastel Blue/ Turquoise
Brow (3rd Eye)	Violet	Lavender
Crown	White / Indigo	Silver

Some people don't need to go through the process of bringing down the fourth and fifth dimensional chakras because they can naturally reach the necessary vibrations. If this is the case for you then fine. I am doing this the long way for those who will benefit from it. With time and practice you'll be able to raise your body's vibrations and go directly to the fifth dimension to connect to the angels. If you are a healer then you most probably have already reached those levels. But it is still a lovely experience and I hope you enjoy it.

Before we go to the fourth dimension to meet your spirit guide and loved ones, spend a few moments asking yourself who you would like to meet, preparing some questions for your guide and loved ones.

Visualisation

Breathe deeply and with one deep out-breath push your roots down deep into the ground and with your next out-breath, breathe out all the fear and negativity, opening all your chakras, expanding your aura and pressing your thumb and first finger together. Know that you are fully open and protected.

You find yourself standing on a hill just above a beach. Looking out over the ocean you see a small island in the distance and dolphins playing in the water. It's to this island that we are going to meet your spirit guide and loved ones.

So, as you stand above the beach notice some steps going down and down to the beach and as you begin to go down the steps feel yourself becoming more and more relaxed. With each step you take you become more and more relaxed, as you go down and down and down onto the beach. Feel the beach under your feet. Feel the breeze and the sun. Notice what you notice about the beach. Can you smell the ocean as you walk gently across the beach towards the sea?

And as you feel the sea lapping gently at your feet notice the dolphins playing and as you enter the water one dolphin in particular comes towards you. This is your special dolphin which will lead you to the island.

Allow yourself to go deeper into the water, knowing that your dolphin in there to protect and support you. Hold on to its fin and allow yourself to move gently through the water towards the island. Feel the sun on your back and sense the water flowing over your body washing away all fear and negativity. Washing away everything that needs to be washed away.

You notice the island is coming closer and closer as your dolphin brings you closer and closer to shore. Know that your dolphin is going to be there to take you back safely but for now begin to leave the water and you feel the beach beneath your feet as you go up onto the island. Just notice what you notice as you move across the beach onto a grassy meadow overlooking the sea.

Spend some time in the meadow exploring. Notice what flowers there are, notice the breeze. Notice what smells there are on this very special island. Sit on your island in the meadow noticing what there is to notice.

If you are taping this then leave a few minutes

Now you begin to realise that there are seven balls of light above your head. These are the fourth dimensional chakras that you are going to bring down into your body to raise your vibration to the fourth dimension to go on the journey to meet your guide and your loved ones.

So notice the first colour, a deep magenta but whatever colour you see and feel is what's right for you. Breathe that ball of light down, down through your crown and into your base allowing the third dimensional chakras to go down through your legs and into the ground.

As you breathe in the fourth dimensional sacrum chakra, coloured peach, breathe it into the sacrum. With it comes the gold of the fourth dimensional solar plexus. And as you breathe in the violet pink of the fourth dimensional heart chakra, feel your heart expand with unconditional love. As you breathe in the violet blue of the fourth dimensional throat chakra, feel your body beginning to vibrate at a higher level. As you breathe in the lavender of the third eye, feel your third eye open wider, and as you breath in the silver ball of light of the fourth dimensional crown chakra know that your body is vibrating at a new level, at the fourth dimensional level. Feel the vibration.

Now off to one side you notice a path, this path will lead you to your loved ones and your spirit guide. So begin to follow this path wherever it leads, knowing it is taking you to a very special place.

Notice what kind of path it is, is it wide or narrow? Is it rocky, does it go through woods or out in the open. Notice what kind of obstacles might be on the path. How do you move around these obstacles? And as you follow the path you might be going higher and higher or lower and lower but wherever it's going is right for you.

If you are taping then leave 5 minutes for the journey

In the distance you see a bend and you know that as you turn this bend in the path you'll see a house and a garden and in the garden will be all your loved ones waiting to receive you. Notice who is there, some you may know, some you may sense you know from past lives. Spend some time with your loved ones. Talk to them in your imagination.

If you are taping this then leave a few minutes to talk to your loved ones.

Now it's time to approach the house. What kind of house is it, a grand mansion, a small cottage, a house you know from your past... what kind of house is it? Does it have many large windows or just a few small ones? What kind of door does it have?

And as you approach the house be aware that your guide is opening the door and waiting to greet you. What do you sense about your guide, what kind of person, male or female? What do they look like, what kind of energy do they represent? If you can't see your guide, ask whether you can give them a face and a name. Use your imagination and whatever you imagine is what is.

Talk to your guide; ask them what information they have to give you at this time in your life that will help you move forward on your journey. What do you need to know right now? Feel your guide's energy and pressing your thumb and second finger together know that whenever you do this in the future you will be back in this space in the presence of your guide. Continue your conversation with your guide.

If you are taping this then leave a few minutes to talk to your guide.

Your guide has a gift for you. It may be an object it may be a word or it may be a symbol. Know that this gift is given in love to help you on your journey. So receive this gift and prepare to leave your guide and your loved ones. Say thank you to your guide and know that you can return to this space at any time in the future, just by pressing your thumb and second finger together.

But for now, letting go of your thumb and second finger, begin to walk back down the path. Notice whether the path is easier now, what may have changed about the path, as you gently go back along the path to the meadow on the island.

Feel the sun on your face, smell the air and notice your dolphin waiting in the water to carry you back to shore. So allow yourself to let go of the fourth dimensional chakras, letting the colours float up and out of your crown and letting the third dimensional chakras come back into your body, watching the colours of the fourth dimensional chakras disappear, as the white of the crown comes back into your body, the violet of the third eye and the blue of the throat. The pink and green of the heart, the yellow of the solar plexus, the orange of the sacrum and the red of the base.

As you return to the water you feel light hearted, refreshed and confident about your future. See your dolphin waiting in the water. Enter the water, hold onto its fin and allow your dolphin to carry you back across the sea. If you wish you can spend some time playing with your dolphin and the other dolphins knowing that again you can return to this space at any time in the future in your imagination and rest and play with the dolphins.

If you are taping this then leave a couple of minutes to play with the dolphins

Now it's time to return to the mainland, so say thank you to the dolphins for watching over you and keeping you safe, as you allow your dolphin to take you back to the beach. As you come back up onto the beach feel the ground beneath your feet and feel the sun drying your body as you move back up to the steps. Coming back up and up and up the steps up to the place where you started with a view of the island. And now, as you look out over the island, feeling yourself open and fully protected let go of your thumb and first finger and begin to close yourself down. Breathing out all the chakra colours, pushing them down and down, deep into the earth, sealing your aura in that seal of protection, bringing up your roots so that you are fully closed and protected. And now begin to wriggle your toes and your fingers and come back into the room.

Now write some detailed notes and drawings of your journey and your house. See the questions below to help you remember. Just allow it to flow from your unconscious.

What was the path like? Wide, narrow, rocky, smooth, straight, or winding?
Did it go up or down?
Did you go through woods, open country, hillsides?
At what different stages did it change?

What type of country did you go through?
What were the obstacles?
How did you get round them? Did you go over, round, under?
How did you feel at the various stages of your journey along your path?
What colours are you using to draw this journey?
What emotions are being raised in you as you do so?

Who was in the garden?
What did they have to say?
How did you feel in the garden with your loved ones?
What type of garden was it?

What type of house was your house, a mansion, cottage, a place you knew or an unknown place?
Was it light, or dark?
What was it made from, brick, stone, mud, thatch, glass, crystal?

How big were the rooms?
How many of them?
Did anyone else live there?

What did you talk about with your guide?
What information did it give you?
What kind of person was your guide? Male, female, old, young, did you recognise them? If you did not see them, go back into their energy and imagine now what they are like, just answer the questions spontaneously, whatever first comes into your mind. Or draw a picture if you wish, just flowing with it, just allow it to come.

What era and culture did they come from? Egyptian, Roman, Native America, Chinese?
What was their name?
What did they look like?

What does this all mean to you?

Guardian Angels

Guardian angels are from the most prolific level of angels. It's part of the angels' evolutionary progress to act as your guardian angel. They are appointed to you and will be with you through the whole of your soul's lifetime, through all your various lifetimes – however many reincarnations you may have. They know you very well and love you unconditionally. They are in charge of your soul's purpose, the quality you are here to bring to the world. By the end of this book you'll know what this is.

Your guardian angels are with you constantly but, as with other angels, under universal law they are not allowed to interfere in your life unless you ask them to. The only thing they can do is to save your life if it's not your souls choice to leave this realm yet. This is why you hear of such wonderful angel encounters and there are many inspirational books written on this subject. You could jump off a cliff and survive if your soul did not want to pass at that time. But everything else you have to ask for.

It's your guardian angel that communicates with you most of the time. Whenever you ask a question it will be your guardian angel who supplies the answer, either by bringing in other angels or by ensuring you notice the white feather, draw a card with your answer, open the right page of a book, or listen to the person they send into your life. When they have communicated in whichever way they can it is still entirely up to you whether you act on the information or not. If you choose not to they will gently keep sending you reminders and signs until you do. They never lose patience, never get cross with you, never feel you are useless. They just keep sending you more love and signs. These may come in dreams as well as in the physical world.

Dreams

Dreams are an important tool that your guardian angel uses to communicate with you. Your angel communicates with your higher self, your soul, and this information filters directly to your inner knowing, your inner wisdom. If you are well connected to your inner wisdom, and you will become more so as you progress, then you trust it and know what you need to do. If you are not so in tune with your intuition then the information is given to you by your unconscious mind in symbolic form. Angels and guides tend to use symbols rather than language. Symbology crosses all cultures, all languages, all time.

There are many dream interpretation books on the market but a dream is yours. If a dream contains a message from your guardian angel, it is your own interpretation of any symbols that is most important. Symbols work on many levels and it is what feels right and resonates with you that matters.

The first symbol I ever received from my guardian angel when I first connected was an equal lateral cross and circle which is the oldest symbol known and represents so many different things. The circle was originally the first symbol of the sun and moon and these are life giving and revered by early civilisations. The 'quarters' are the four archangels protecting the four corners of the earth and the universe. The cross depicts the line of the horizon and the sun as it moves from east to west and also the four directions of the wind. They also represent the four elements earth, air, fire and water.

The Fifth Dimension

In the following meditation we will be changing the vibrational frequency of your chakras yet again, this time to the fifth dimension and bringing down higher chakras to achieve this. As with the last meditation, whatever colours you receive are right for you now and again they may change as you progress through the exercises and your life. There may be higher levels yet to come down and for all you know your soul is already at these levels and may be seeing other colours. Or you are rising at your own pace and the colours will change as you go.

Here are the colours I received:

Chakra	3rd dimension colour	4th dimension color (Pastels)	5th dimension color (silvery crystalline)
Base	Red	Magenta	Platinum
Sacrum	Orange	Peach	Magenta
Solar plexus	Yellow	Gold	Rainbow Gold
Heart	Green/Magenta	Violet Pink	White
Throat	Blue/Turquoise	Violet Blue	Royal Blue
Brow (3rd eye)	Violet	Lavender	Silver Violet
Crown	White/Indigo	Silver	Crystalline Gold

Your guardian angel will present itself to you in some way or other. You may not see anything but you'll be aware of an energy. If you try too hard to see or sense your angel, you can block yourself. Just relax and trust that your angel will be there. It may take you three or four attempts before you sense anything, so be patient. Remember that you can actively use your imagination. Whatever you imagine whilst doing this exercise will be real. That is why you are imagining things. The more actively you use your imagination the more real the experience.

There is no right or wrong way to connect to your guardian angel for the first time. You need to be comfortable and relaxed, with your body well supported. I like to play some soft music in the background, light a candle and burn some incense or oil, usually frankincense but any relaxing aroma you like will do. If you use the same aroma each time then after a while you'll just need to smell the aroma to be in the state and invoke the feelings you'll experience during the journey.

First find some time when you'll be undisturbed. Remove the telephone from the receiver to ensure no interruptions. Allow approximately half and hour for the first time you do the exercise. If you are new to meditation and visualisation you may need to practice a bit.

Journey to Meet your Guardian Angel

So, begin to focus on your breathing and as you breathe out, breathe those roots deep into the ground, anchoring yourself. As you breathe in, feel the energy coming up, opening all your chakras and tumbling down around your head protecting you. As you press your thumb and first finger together know that you are fully open and fully protected.

As you press your thumb and second finger together feel yourself on your island with your guide at the fourth dimension knowing that you are now going on a journey to the fifth dimension where your guardian angel awaits.

Now find yourself standing in the garden of your house and over to one side see, feel or hear a golden escalator going up and up into the sky. As you stand at the bottom of the escalator with your guide notice the fifth dimensional chakras in a line above your head and know that these chakras will help take you to the fifth dimension.

So, as you go up the golden escalator allow these colours of light to enter your crown, letting the fourth dimensional chakras go down into the earth. See or feel the platinum chakra of the fifth dimension coming down into your base.

Now breathe in the magenta chakra and have it come down into your sacrum.

As you breathe in the rainbow gold of the fifth dimensional chakra into your solar plexus, feel your body begin to vibrate at a new level.

As you pull down the pure white of the fifth dimensional heart chakra, feel the unconditional love of the universe fill your heart and go out to the world.

As you breathe down the royal blue of the throat chakra, know that all is well with you.

As you breathe down the silver violet of the fifth dimensional third eye chakra, become aware of your expanding awareness.

And as you bring down the crystalline gold of the crown chakra be aware that you are one with all things. Be aware of the golden escalator taking you higher and higher and you are feeling lighter and lighter and floating out into the golden web of the universal energy that connects all things.

As you notice the web of energy surrounding you, off into the distance you see a crystal temple and you hear the most beautiful music. This is the most beautiful place you have ever experienced and as you float across the web towards the temple know that your guardian angel is waiting to meet you.

Go up the steps of the crystal temple, feel the cool smooth crystal beneath your feet, hear the music playing and notice your guardian angel waiting for you. As you approach, feel the unconditional love of your guardian angel surrounding you, fulfilling you, and as you feel and experience this energy, press your thumb and third finger together, so that you can return to this place and at any time in the future.

What type of energy is your angel? Does it have any particular colour or form? What other quality may it be bringing you right now? Notice this.

Now spend some time with your guardian angel, talking, finding out maybe what's the purpose of this lifetime and what you might need to cut away from in your life at present to allow you to move forward.

If you are taping then leave 5 minutes to talk to your guardian angel.

Now it is time to leave your guardian angel but know that you can return to this place at any time in the future just by pressing your thumb and third finger together; and know that your guardian angel is always with you and will be returning with you.

So as you leave the temple be aware that you are crossing the universe, crossing part of the golden web. And as you return down the golden escalator, which brings you back down and down to the fourth dimension, you let go of the fifth dimensional chakra colours. (Now let go with your thumb and third finger). And as you feel or see the fourth dimensional chakras come back into your body – silver for the crown, the lavender for the third eye, the violet blue for the throat, and the violet pink for the heart, the gold for the solar plexus, and the peach of the sacrum, and the magenta for the base, press your thumb and second finger together. Come back down, down on the golden escalator and find yourself back in the garden with your guide and your loved ones.

As you return back down along the path know that you can return at any time to meet your guide and loved ones or your guardian angel just by pressing your thumb and second finger or third finger together.

But for now come back down the path, back to the meadow on the island and notice the fourth dimensional chakras floating back out of the top of your head as the third dimensional chakras come back into your body.

The pure white of the crown, the purple of the third eye, the blue of the throat, the green and pink of the heart, the yellow of the solar plexus, the orange of the sacrum and the red of the base. And letting go of your thumb and your second finger as you return to the water, notice that your dolphin is waiting to take you back; back across the ocean and to the mainland and back to the beach from where you started. Know that you can return to these places at any time in the future.

And as you cross the beach and go up the steps to where you started, press your thumb and first finger together. And as you look over at the island, begin to close yourself down, breathing out all the chakra colours, pushing them down deep into the earth, feeling your aura and your protection and letting go of your thumb and first finger. Now bring up your roots so that you are fully closed and protected.

Begin to wriggle your toes and your fingers and come back into the room.

Write and draw your experiences in your journal.

What was your temple like?

What was your angel like?

What did you talk about?

What did it say?

What symbol did it give you?

What does this all mean to you?

PART II YOUR JOURNEY

CHAPTER 5

Sandolphon

Starting

Now we start our journey with the angels. Working through the chakras to cleanse, balance and heal yourself of any deep-seated issues, any negative belief patterns, and reactive behaviours that no longer serve you. You are beginning a lifetime journey of getting closer to yourself, being more of the divine person you really are, and becoming closer to the angels and our creator.

It's important for all the chakras to be energised and functioning efficiently for the all-round well being of the individual on all levels, physical, mental, emotional and spiritual. What's wrong in the physical body may be a reflection of something wrong in one or more of the other bodies. Clearing the chakras regularly leads to better health on all levels.

You can do all these exercises over and over again, at different times in your life. The more you do them, the more you'll clear, and the more you clear, the more you open yourself up to your own inner wonderful self. The closer you feel to the divine.

As you have discovered, as you go through the dimensions your chakras and vibrations change. On this course we are focussing on clearing the third dimension because this is the dimension we live at on a day to day basis and it is these chakras that store our traumas from this life. Past life traumas are held in the fourth and fifth dimensional chakras, which is why we are in altered states of consciousness whilst connected to angels and doing this work.

Root Chakra (One)

Location	Perineum, base of spine, coccyx, between legs
Colour	Red
Developmental Age	0 – 3 years
Sense	Smell
Glands / organs	Adrenals, kidneys, spinal column, colon, legs, bones
Concerns	Survival, security, belonging, being here and now, support
Out of Balance	Fear, overly concerned with material security. Jungle mentality. Feeling unsafe, lack of security, no sense of belonging. Vague, airy-fairy-not-really-here people.
Body Symptoms	Problems in kidneys, rectum, hips, bowel spasm, piles, colitis, chrone's disease, constipation. Lower back problems, and tension in the spine.
Qualities / Lessons	Matters relating to the material world, success. The physical body, mastery of the body, grounding, individuality, stability, security, stillness, health, courage, patience.
Negative Qualities	Overly concerned with one's physical survival. Self-centred, violence, greed, anger, insecurity.
Positive Qualities	Self-control, common sense, individuality, patience, vitality, survival instincts
Soul Issue	To acknowledge the soul inhabits a body that is part of the living universe. Through the body the soul is brought into matter.
Element	Earth
Gems & Minerals	Ruby, garnet, bloodstone, red jasper, black tourmaline, obsidian, smoky quartz.
Associated Angels	Archangel Sandolphon, Uriel, Angels of the Earth.
Associated Oils	Benzoine, patchouli, vetivert

Archangel Sandolphon

For this chakra we shall be working with Archangel Sandolphon. He is one of only two angels who were once mortal. It is said that he was the prophet

 Elijah and God elevated him to an angel. He is said to be so tall that he actually connects heaven and earth which is why he is often associated with the tree of life. This is said to be why he is so connected to earth and mankind interceding on behalf of people and delivering their prayers to God and bringing the responses. Like the other angels, he sends messages in dreams, imagination, feathers, and fleeting wispy thoughts that flit across the consciousness. He is also said to help parents determine the gender of forthcoming children.

Connecting to Archangel Sandolphon will help you release any insecurity issues you have in relation to being alive and living your life to the full. For instance, perhaps your happiness depends on someone else. This is not necessarily good for a relationship. You don't wish to be reliant on this person for fear of them leaving will affect your ability to live a full life. If you are dependent on someone you can sometimes feel a burden to them and this can cause resentment and the eventual breakdown of a relationship if you are not careful. Notice if there is a physical cord between you and if so use the cutting cords exercise with Archangel Michael and Gabriel in Chapter 9 then re-grow an etheric cord of unconditional love, heart to heart, so you are both free independent individuals. You can do this after this current exercise or whenever it feels right for you.

Sandolphon is about cycles, there is always new life and death at each and every part of the year. It is important to give yourself time to grow. New seeds need to be planted and given time to germinate and grow. Last year's dead wood needs to be cut out and the ground prepared first. Sandolphon responds to working with the cycles of nature. Look at nature and connect to the wonders of our own Mother Earth. Send healing to Mother Earth to replenish everything man removes, and the damage we as humans do to our planet. For any of these things Sandolphon will be the angel to connect to and who will assist you.

Remember it is the quality of energy you are connecting to. For instance, many people want to win the lottery. But it's more about what the lottery means and what it will bring into your life. For me the lottery represents security, but for others it may be power or freedom. But if I ask to feel more secure this can come in many ways rather than just the lottery. Sandolphon is the angel to help you feel more secure, so asking him into your life assures you of receiving what you need.

We shall also connect to the base chakra and ask Sandolphon to clear any blockages. Many blockages related to security issues can reside in the base chakra, especially if there were any difficulties during birth, or near fatal accidents or illnesses prior to three years old. These events can leave an unconscious fear of living and of really committing to enjoying life.

Exercise: Choosing the Issue to Work With

Before connecting to Archangel Sandolphon, there is an exercise to help you find or choose the issue you might need to work with at this time. Ask yourself these questions and write in your journal everything that comes to mind. These are issues that could affect your base chakra.

Did you suffer from any very early trauma, eg. a difficult birth, that may affect your will to survive?

Where you adopted?

Ask yourself: How were the first three years of my life?

Did I feel protected and supported?

Why might I have chosen my parents and this particular culture for this lifetime?

Am I afraid to live?

Do you question the value of your life, or of life in general?

Do you feel you belong here on this planet?

Do you dissociate yourself from the present moment perhaps by daydreaming, floating outside yourself, emotionally, psychologically or even mentally?

Do you think and analyse your way into making things seem exactly how you want them to be?

Do you worry excessively about survival or security?

Do you get angry easily?

Are you attached to external things like your home, your environment, your family, possessions, money?

Do you rely on someone for your sense of security?

What do you feel you need?

Do you suffer from panic attacks, back problems, IBS (irritable bowel syndrom), kidney troubles, constipation?

Do you need to slow down?

Do you need to be more grounded?

Do you feel like an outsider within groups or your family?

Are you afraid of letting go of control?

Draw a picture of what you feel your base chakra might look like. What might be blocking it. Use whatever colours come to you. Notice the emotions and feelings that come up in you as you do this, write them down and let them go.

Now look at what you have drawn or written. Did you scribble, did you feel angry, sad, happy, frustrated, what were the feelings doing these exercises brought up in you?

What have you learned about yourself answering these questions and doing these exercises?

Now pick any issue or group of issues to work with on this occasion. What might you want to let go of and what might you want to bring into your life?

If you don't have any definitive answers to the above, don't worry.

Within the meditation Archangel Sandolphon will bring the necessary information. Whatever you do in your imagination is as effective as doing it for real, according to scientific research from America. Even if you have no idea what's necessary, it will still happen as long as you use your imagination.

Connecting to Archangel Sandolphon

In the last chapter I gave you some tips on connecting quickly to specific angels. If you have been practicing this then you'll have no trouble with working through the remainder of the chapters. If not, then take your time preparing for each visualisation. Go through the exercise in Chapter 3, climbing through the dimensions and going with your guardian angel to meet each angel as we go through the coming chapters.

The easiest way to connect to Archangel Sandolphon is through prayer. He is the angel of prayer. Ensure you have at least half and hour where you'll be undisturbed, put on some music to help you relax. All the angels love music but Sandolphon does in particular. I usually light an oil burner with patchouli oil, (but make sure the candle/tea-light is safe).

Sit quietly, hold one of the crystals mentioned in the base chakra chart and focus on the quality you want to ask for. If you have a fear of life or death, whether you wish to feel more secure as a person, or in your profession, if you wish to plant new seeds for growth next year, or if you need general guidance on any base chakra issues. For the purposes of this exercise I shall use general security but you may substitute something more appropriate for you if you wish.

When you are clear in your mind as to what it is you need to bring to Archangel Sandolphon, and after having pressed your thumb and first finger together to open and protected yourself, and your thumb and second finger to take you to the fourth dimension, and your thumb and third finger to take you to the fifth dimension, then breathe deeply, allow yourself to relax and find yourself in a place in nature. Somewhere on earth, it can be a favourite place or an imaginary place, somewhere you feel safe and secure. Notice if there is anyone with you, someone you rely on, someone you feel secure with.

Begin to focus your attention on praying from the heart, with your emotions, and you are asking Archangel Sandolphon to come and be with you. You are praying from the peace within your heart that Sandolphon be with you and assist you in cleansing your base chakra and allowing you to feel more secure in life. Invoke him by repeating his name three times, Sandolphon, Sandolphon, Sandolphon. Allow yourself to feel his presence, know that he his there, take some time to notice, what do you sense, how do you feel, what do you smell, what might you see; use all your senses. Be aware that his loving energy is around you. Take a few moments to really become aware of Sandolphon's energy so you can tell it from other angelic energies.

(If you are taping this leave a pause of about two minutes...)

Now ask Archangel Sandolphon to help you let go of your issue and cleanse your base chakra. Gently begin to focus on your base chakra see and sense what colour it is, bright red, murky, even brown, sense how fast it might be spinning, does it feel really wide open or only just open. See or sense the issue in whatever form it takes within your base chakra. See or sense what blockage it may be causing ask your chakra in your mind what it needs, what it might need to let go of. Be aware of any thoughts, feelings, reflections, memories there may or may not be.

(If you are taping this leave a pause of about 2 minutes)

Ask Archangel Sandolphon to draw out any murky colours, see or sense them leaving your chakra, floating gently up into the air, being drawn out by Archangel Sandolphon up out of your aura into the air into the angelic realms to be transformed back into positive energy. Ask Archangel Sandolphon to cleanse your base chakra with pure red light, feel the red light coming down through your crown, down your body and flooding your base chakra.

(If you are taping this leave a pause of a minute)

Imagine yourself letting go of any fears or insecurities you may feel about yourself, your career, your relationships, whatever is right for you, and your life in general. Be as specific or general as you wish, whatever comes to you is what's right for you. Whatever your experience, know that it is just right for you at this time. As the bright red light is shining into your base chakra, you see and sense your chakra clearing and becoming clear and bright, fully open and spinning freely. As you do so feel yourself become more and more secure, more and more happy with your life, know that you are here for a purpose, whatever that purpose may be, know that you are letting go of whatever fears have been holding you back from moving forward and enjoying your life.

Then, when you feel that your chakra can't hold any more red light, know you are truly cleansed and balanced and allow the light to fade away.

Know that Sandolphon is with you, that your base chakra is cleansed and balanced and you are ready to move forward in your life. Be aware that you have let go of many past issues, either consciously or unconsciously and that you are preparing the way for a new and wonderful life.

Thank Archangel Sandolphon for his help in clearing your base chakra, for making you feel more secure and paving the way for a new you. Let Archangel Sandolphon float away back into the heavens and be aware you can call on him at any time in the future just by saying your prayers. Now letting go of your thumb and third finger, and your thumb and second finger, to bring yourself back to the third dimension and now let go of your thumb and first finger to close yourself down and gently bring yourself back into the room. Move your fingers and toes and having a glass of water to ensure you are fully back and grounded again.

Make notes of your experience and how you are currently feeling in comparison to how you felt before the exercise in your journal or draw a picture of the two.

What have you learned from this experience, from this chapter?
How are you going to be different in the future?
What are you going to do differently?

Replenishing Earth Energy

A quick and simple thing you can also do with Archangel Sandolphon is to allow yourself to act as a channel for him to send healing energy to the planet. Whenever you are open, for instance at the end of any exercise, just allow yourself to feel the energy coming down through your crown and out through your feet, sending energy to mother earth to replenish her for everything we, as mankind, take out of her.

You can do this with any angel but it works particularly well with Sandolphon and Raphael. You can also hold any round object to represent the earth in your hands and allow yourself to feel the energy coming out of your hands and into the object. Know that the energy is going into the earth.

The first time I did this I used a rugby ball, holding it upright with one end on the floor and my hands holding the ball up. I thought of all the different ways in which mankind poisons our earth and the damage we have done to our planet. I felt very humble and was asking for forgiveness on behalf of mankind, for not originally knowing any better. The amount of energy that channelled through was amazing. Most probably the strongest vibration of energy I have ever felt in my career. It was a fantastic experience. Try it for yourselves.

Sending Healing to Troubled Areas on the Planet

You can also send healing to any region of the world that needs it, either by the power of your intention or with the use of props. For instance, if you have a globe or a map you can place your hands on an area and focus the energy that way. If not just imagine the energy going to wherever you feel it is needed. This benefits everyone in those areas.

Many healers did this during the war in Iraq and to the Far East after the tsunami. Healing is constantly being sent to Palestine and Israel. Wherever there is conflict, the healing energy can eventually help to bring about peace to the world. There has been a steady increase in this energy over the years and in the number of people sending energy to the situation in Northern Ireland, and slowly, over the years, it has been taking effect.

The more people engaged in sending loving healing energy to wherever it is needed for the highest good of all concerned, not just one particular faction, the more love and light there will be in the world and the less darkness.

CHAPTER 6

Phuel

In this chapter we will be looking at the second chakra, known as the sacrum chakra. This chakra deals with reproduction, but more importantly self worth.

There are many angels you can work with but we are going to be working with Archangel Phuel, Lord of the Moon which regulates our tides and represents water and emotions.

Location	Lower abdomen, below the navel, the sacrum
Colour	Orange
Developmental Age	2 – 5 or 8 years old
Sense	Taste
Glands / organs	Reproductive system, ovaries, testicles, prostate, genitals, spleen, womb, bladder
Concerns	Intimacy, self-respect, self-worth, sharing, creativity, child-like mystery.
Out of balance	Creative blocks, need to possess another. Fear of intimacy. No sense of mystery and magic.
Body symptoms	Problems related to the reproductive system.
Qualities / lessons	Giving and receiving, emotions, desire, pleasure, sexual/ passionate love, change, movement, assimilation of new ideas, health, family, tolerance, surrender, working with others.
Negative qualities	Promiscuous, anger, hurt, stuck in rut.
Positive qualities	Passion, giving and receiving, sense of family and community with the greater world, creativity.
Soul Issue	To experience intimacy with another with a sense of self-respect. The expression of creative imagination in whatever form.
Element	Water
Gems & Minerals	Carnelian, coral, gold, calcite, amber, citrine, gold topaz,

peach aventurine.

Associated Angels	Archangel Pheul, Chamuel, Angels of Birth, Gabriel, Micah, Fortunata.
Associated Oils	Carrot seed, dill, geranium, hyssop, jasmine, marjoram, neroli, rose, sandalwood.

The Sacrum Chakra (two)

As soon as we are born (arrive on this planet) we start to notice we're not alone. There are others here with us. How we relate to others is learned from our relationships with our primary care givers, family and siblings, and this forms the basis of how we relate to others in later life. These early years form our patterns of behaviour around relationships. This is why so many therapies take you back to childhood and why in so many meditations you start to remember things from your childhood. When you have identified a pattern you can interrupt it and change it for something that is more useful to you now.

This chakra is about movement and flexibility, how we move through our lives. Having learned to let go of the security issues of the base chakra, this is where we learn to explore the world, if we are allowed to. This is when we need to be encouraged to be ourselves and that whatever we feel, whatever we do, we are still loved – even if we are having a temper tantrum. What normally happens is that we a taught that temper tantrums are bad. This means we are bad children for not doing as we are told and exploring our space instead of staying where we have been told. So we learn not to explore our environment. We learn that doing new and interesting things is not 'being good'.

This chakra also holds our views on sexuality and how we relate sexually with others. Some people are brought up within families where sexuality is loving, it is normal. Others where it's considered to be dirty, it's naughty, it's disgusting, or good girls don't do that sort of thing. In most families there will be a mixture of both, usually coming from different generations. But the views of those closest to you will be the ones that affect you most.

Creativity is developed within the sacrum chakra. It is a time when we are very imaginative. Children imagine things and make them real for themselves. It's in this realm where children learn to create. If this is encouraged, you grow, if it's not encouraged, then your creative energy withers on its young shoots and becomes stunted. It never actually dies. Imagination and creativity are one and the same and are right brain functions. As soon as we go to school, life starts to squash the imagination and left brain logical activity is encouraged. There is not even much emphasis any more on other right brain activities such as art, music or dance.

Low self-esteem is often associated with sacrum issues. Parents love their children so much that they can often encourage them and encourage them to work harder, be better, "well done darling but...", until children begin to believe they can do nothing right. They cannot please those they love and there must be something wrong with them, they end up believing they are just not good enough.

This old misconception can carry on and affect later life. Many take on careers because they may have been told they are not clever enough, or not intelligent enough to be whatever it was they wanted to be. They spend their life being unhappy, never believing in themselves and trying so hard to be perfect; to get everything right, to be good enough. If this sounds like you, then have faith. You are good enough, you are a divine being in a human body, just like everyone else, and all you have to be is the best you can be. If you give yourself permission to not be perfect, you give yourself permission to try to be. Many people say that to try and fail is better than to have never tried at all. By giving yourself permission to fail you can take the first step towards your goal, which is further than you would have gone had you not even tried.

Our soul works with us through the chakras and what we need to be aware of is that every significant relationship in our lives gives us the opportunity to look at ourselves at a deeper level. They give us a key to open and look at our relationship with ourselves as well as others. Hopefully we learn to relate to others without the fear of losing them, or the need to manipulate or possess them. As we learn and grow and change, so we let go of the need to attract people into our lives to nurture us and give us the love that may not have been adequately expressed by our families.

One thing to remember about relationships is that invariably we do for others exactly what we want done for ourselves and others do for us exactly what they want done for themselves. I remember a relationship where my partner did everything for me. He wanted to look after me, protect me; he cared for me in every way. It was a mothering experience. Whereas I just wanted as much space and as much independence as I could get. He had received very inadequate mothering as a child, not because his mother didn't love him, but just that she did not know how to express it. No kisses, no cuddles, no playing. His defence – she was very busy. I, on the other hand, had been over-protected by my mother, I was never allowed to do anything, as my safety was my mother's main concern. I had to be the good, pretty little girl she wanted, whereas I was really much more of a tomboy. I could not grow, I learned that being me was wrong, so I just wanted to be alone. So guess what? I gave him as much space as I wanted. The first thing necessary was for us to notice what was happening, the second was for me to realise that I was not being smothered and that I could be myself and still be accepted, and for him to realise I did care, even if I was not as demonstrative as he would have wished. I also had to learn that being demonstrative did not lead to smothering. This was a very rewarding part of my journey.

The sacrum chakra is also about balancing the two energies of the masculine and feminine, which are held within everyone. We are each a mixture of masculine and feminine energy, whatever our gender. Our right brain is associated with feminine energy and governs creativity, our intuition, sixth sense, inner wisdom, our gentler nature, and soul issues, as well as ruling the left hand side of our bodies. Our left brain is regarded as masculine. It governs logic, analytical thought, learning, thinking, reason, ego personality, and rules the right hand side of our body. In our modern culture most emphasis is put on developing this side of our brain and energy. It's important to balance these two sides of our personalities, so that we use all our potential.

Archangel Phuel

I have chosen to work with Archangel Phuel, Lord of the Moon. The moon represents feminine energy. The emotions associated with women and the softer side of our natures, but I sense Phuel as a masculine angel, (even though all angels are androgynous) thus bringing balance to the  chakra. He balances the emotions and brings peace and tranquillity to all. You may sense this angel as feminine – whatever it is, it will represent the energy you are dealing with and need most in your life.

Be aware that there would be no life without water and that life on this planet sprang from water. It has been said that water responds to love and energy (see *The Hidden Messages in Water* by Masaru Emoto), and in some scientific research conducted in America they have proven not only does water have memory that water also exists in space. And, of course, our bodies are between 75 per cent to 80 per cent water.

Think Back to Your Childhood

Using your journal write and draw the thoughts, feelings and any insights that come to you when answering the following questions.

How was your childhood between the ages of 1-5 in relation to how safe you felt?

Were you encouraged to be creative? What happened when you showed someone what you have created? How was it received? With enthusiasm or absent mindedness? How did you feel?

How do you use your creative abilities now?

How do you feel about your sexuality and sex in general?

Do you suffer from impotence or lack of interest in sex?

Do you feel "not good enough" and if so in which areas of your life. Personal relationships, career, finances, mother or fatherhood?

Do you suffer from fluid retention, PMT, lymph drainage problems?

Do you feel rigid in your body, emotions or thoughts?

Do you suffer from illness such as fibromyalga, arthritis, anything that affects your flexibility?

Do you suffer from lower back pain, hips or joint pain?

Now begin to write and draw in your journal what has come up for you at this time. Let go of all judgement, it just is. There is no right or wrong. It just is.

Connecting to Archangel Phuel

By now you'll be very familiar with preparing your space with relaxing music, incense or oils of your choice, ensuring that you have sufficient time and that you are feeling relaxed for a meditation. For Phuel my favourite essential oil is sandalwood. I also usually hold a carnelian crystal. You'll also be familiar with grounding yourself, protecting yourself, opening your chakras and taking yourself to the fifth dimensional frequency by using your anchors of pressing your thumb and fingers together. This will be the starting point for this exercise.

Be aware that although you have taken yourself to the fifth dimension and your chakras have changed colour – the work you are doing will be on the third dimension because it is this life you are working with, so don't be surprised if your sacrum chakra changes colour back to third dimension while you work.

To connect to Phuel for the first time, go to the space where you meet your guardian angel. If you are still not sure what you want to work on take a moment to ask your guardian angel.

(If taping then leave a minute)

Now ask your guardian angel to take you across the universe to Phuel's temple. Imagine yourself being held by your guardian angel floating out into space, across the universal matrix that connects you to everything that is. In the distance you see a beautiful temple made of turquoise crystal. Hear the celestial music playing and know that Archangel Phuel awaits you. He has information for you, which is going to help you move on positively in your life. He will explain what you need to know to let go of a past pattern that is holding you back in your life so you can move forward with more confidence and a greater sense of self.

As you approach the temple your guardian angel drops back to let you enter it. Phuel stands at the far end with his/her arms outstretched to meet you. There are other angels of the moon and water around welcoming you. As you walk/glide towards Phuel you notice an aquamarine crystal couch on which and you are invited to lay down. If the couch is not aquamarine what colour is this couch? Be aware that it is the colour you need most in this sacrum chakra right now. Archangel Phuel surrounds you and the couch with his/her wings. You are safely enfolded in these angelic wings and you feel so much love. Rest in this space and feel Archangel Phuel's energy. Get to know the quality of this energy, is it soft or hard, determined or gentle? Is it warm or cold, what colours do you see? What words come into your consciousness with this energy? What do you see, hear, smell? Do you taste something, what does it remind you of? What is this energy? How are you going to know this energy again?

(If you are taping this meditation, leave a pause of about three minutes…)

Become aware of how Phuel is communicating with you. Is it with pictures and visions? Do you hear a voice in your head? Do you pick up feelings in your body? Are you getting thoughts in your mind? Or is it a little of each? Be aware of how Phuel is communicating with you and how your body best communicates with you.

(If you are taping pause a minute or so)

As you lie on the couch be aware that the crystal couch connects to your sacrum chakra and brings forward memories and emotions that need to be brought to your consciousness to be cleansed and let go. Spend some time with Phuel on the crystal couch becoming aware of what past patterns you need to let go of in your life right now. Thinking about where they come from, how they were formed, respect them and thank them for the positive elements they brought to your life, how they protected the younger you.

(If taping leave a pause of about three minutes ...)

Now start to ask Archangel Phuel for help. What is your learning from this situation; how are you going to go forward in the future; what do you need to do for yourself; how are you going to take responsibility from now on? How is Phuel going to help you? What do you need to do next, which direction is the right direction for you right now? Be aware of this information coming to you even if you are not aware of the content of all the information, know that it is being absorbed at an unconscious level and on a cellular level in your body and it will come to into consciousness at the perfect time in the future when you need it.

(If taping leave about three minutes pause...)

Now be aware of Archangel Phuel aiming a beam of light straight into your sacrum chakra. This light may be the same colour or different from the colour of the couch – be aware it is the light you need right now. Feel the chakra being cleansed.

(If taping leave one minute)

Now feel Archangel Phuel and the other angels leading you to a crystal clear pool full of warm or cool clear water. As you enter the pool be aware of all old unnecessary emotions being cleansed from your body, and feel the water caress your body, washing away whatever negative emotions are there. Allow yourself to feel the water and let go. If you are feeling nothing, just be aware that all negative emotions are being washed away and you are letting go. Let go, let go. Let go of anything you no longer need right now. Now become aware of your body and your chakra. What colour is it now, is it clear, spinning, is it different, is it spinning differently, more smoothly, in an opposite direction? How is this chakra responding to Archangel Phuel's healing? What kind of creative endeavours are you going to bring into your life in the future? How is Phuel going to help you develop your creativity?

(If taping leave one minute)

Now be aware that Archangel Phuel has done all he can at present but that you can return to this place at any time in the future and that you can call Archangel Phuel to you wherever you are for help with any form of emotional or sexual issues. Come out of the pool and feel Phuel dry you with his/her wings. Thank Archangel Phuel for the information and the healing you have received. Know that you can return at any time. Now feel your guardian angel come to you and lead you gently out of the temple, back, back, across the universe back to where you began.

Then very gently, when you are ready, begin to let go of your anchors, letting go of the fifth dimension, the fourth dimension, feeling yourself closed and protected and very gently bring yourself back into your body, by wiggling your toes, and your fingers before gently opening your eyes.

Now, write or draw your experiences in your journal. Then reflect on what you have drawn. What other messages may be held in this? What else have you learned about yourself right now?

CHAPTER 7

Uriel and Ramaela

In this chapter we will be focusing on Archangel Uriel and the solar plexus chakra. There are many angels that work with the issues within this chakra and at the end of this chapter I will give you details of the others so that you can work with some of them in the future. As you'll notice, many angels work with more than one chakra. This is because everything is inter-related.

The reason there are so many angels working with the solar plexus is because it is our emotional powerhouse and many emotional conflicts get stored there.

By spending time clearing and balancing this chakra you are beginning the process of regaining your own authority and power.

After we have made this start, we will then invoke Archangel Ramaela to bring her into your life. She is the angel of Laughter and Joy, which are two very important qualities in helping you create a happy and healthy life.

Solar Plexus Chakra (Three)

Location	Solar Plexus, above the navel, below the chest.
Colour	Yellow
Developmental Age	6 – 12 years
Sense	Sight
Glands / organs	Pancreas, adrenals, stomach, liver, gallbladder, nervous system, muscles.
Concerns	Self worth, determination, identify personal power.
Out of balance	Self-centred, no sense of identity, powerless, need to control, need to take care of others.
Body symptoms	Diabetes, liver disease, ulcers, problems with stomach, spleen and small intestine.
Qualities / lessons	Will, personal power, authority, energy, mastery of desire, self-control. Radiance, warmth, wakening, transformation, humour, laughter, immortality.

Negative qualities	Taking in more than one can assimilate. Too much emphasis on power and or recognition. Anger, fear, hate, digestive problems.
Positive qualities	Vision, selfless service, balanced ego, leadership, energy, charisma, self-motivation.
Soul Issue	To experience a sense of self worth, self empowerment and purpose.
Element	Fire
Gems & Minerals	Citrine, gold topaz, amber, tiger's eye, gold calcite, gold, angelite.
Associated Angels	Archangel Uriel, Archangel Michael, Jophiel, Ramaela, Fortunata, Phuel, Micah.
Associated Oils	Benzoine, bergamot, black pepper, chamomile, clary sage, cypress, dill, elemi, fennel, hyssop, juniper, lemon, marjoram, neroli, palmarosa, sage.

Our divine being (spirit/soul) is pure loving energy, and we choose to incarnate as a human being to experience ourselves. The only way we can experience our life is through our bodies. Our feelings and emotions are experienced through our body, not through our mind.

I tend to think of our mind as being everything we have learnt since birth, like an empty computer hard disc that collects all our experiences both good and bad and stores them away for future reference. But like a computer, bits of information get scrambled and linked to the wrong things and filed in strange places, and every so often we need to de-frag and build new more appropriate links.

All this old information is formed in childhood and becomes our belief patterns, what we believe about ourselves, our family. For instance, if parents keep saying "well done, but..." we end up feeling we are not good enough. So if in childhood you learned that you could never get your own way, you could end up feeling you can do nothing, you can achieve nothing and you are powerless. You store these feelings in your solar plexus. You can't change the world, you can't change other people, but you can change how you choose to view and experience your life. You can change how you behave and react to life if you choose.

Our body is our direct connection to the universe. It's through our bodies that we experience our lives and it's through our bodies that the universe, spirit, the angels and our higher selves communicate with us. Our Chakras connect to our body and to universal energy. They are the gateway if you like.

The solar plexus is the emotional powerhouse of our body. It develops particularly between 6 years old and 12 years old. These are often very difficult years both for parents and children. This is when a child begins to develop its own power or feelings of powerlessness.

Children whose parents are over protective, or who don't allow them to develop their own decision making process, may find themselves quite indecisive later in life.

If events outside our control happen to us it can leave a lasting drive to be in complete and absolute control of our life. This, of course, is not possible, we can't control outside events, but we can choose how we feel, how we experience our life. Do we look at life as an exciting adventure (like young children do) or do we fear the unexpected.

How do you view change in your life? As exciting, an opportunity to learn, to grow, to experience new things, to have fun? Or as something to be feared and avoided at all costs? Or, if not avoided then to be controlled. Do you control your life and try and make it go in one direction, or do you take the opportunities to explore new places, new horizons and new ideas?

The journey of life is just that, a journey. You can go down the motorway or you can explore all the side roads and villages along the way. You can stop and rest in service stations with food that tastes the same the world over, or discover little hotels and pubs down a country lane that might end by a lake, the sea, a cliff top, a meadow. Taking the side roads may lead to some dead ends and back tracking but what experiences and what fun you will have. You still get to the same place in the end. And personally I don't want to get there too soon.

Exercise

Look at the solar plexus chart and see what relates to you. If you are not sure, ask yourself the following questions, write your answers in your journal and see what comes up for you. You can use this exercise as many times as you like. You'll find that as you look at the questions over and over, slowly your answers will change and you'll be able to review your progress from your journal. This is a lifetime journey. Reviewing your progress will encourage you.

Do you have any recurring health issues in any areas listed above? This can also point you in the direction of where any issues are being held. I used to get an awful lot of indigestion because there was a lot in my life, and about myself, that I could not stomach. Now that I am feeling happier with my life and myself, after much work and help from the angels, my indigestion has cleared up. If I ever get indigestion now, which is not often, I look carefully to see what area of my life might be causing it (… after, of course, I have made sure I have not been over indulging, and if so, I would look to see what caused me to over indulge in the first place).

So ask yourself:

1   Are you a people pleaser, do you put others' needs before your own?

2   Are you always worrying about what others will think or feel?

3   How often do you say 'No' to others and 'Yes' to yourself when you feel this is needed, or do you find it is invariably the other way round?

4   Do you feel guilty if you please yourself?

5   Do you know what does please you?

6   Can you appreciate someone else's point of view that is different from your own and accept it as different, or do you feel the need to make them accept your point of view?

7   Do you get angry if they don't listen and understand you?

8   Are you aware of your emotions? How do you respond to them?

9   Do you experience them or do you push them away and bury them?

10 What situations make you feel threatened?

11 What situations make you feel vulnerable?

12 Are you stubborn? If so, who or what pushes those buttons and puts you in stubborn mode?

13 Can you relate it to your past and choose another form of behaviour that will get you what you want?

14 Can you express your emotions calmly and honestly to others or do you keep things to yourself?

15 Do you actually know how you feel about things?

For instance, you are going on holiday. Your family wants you to go with them to the same place as always. You want to go somewhere else either alone or with friends. How do you feel? (Not, what do you *think*, but how do your *feel*?) You might feel a variety of feelings. You might feel flat and heavy in your body at the thought of going with your parents again. You might feel scared or excited or both at the thought of going away on your own. You might feel scared of telling your parents you don't want to go with them, you may fear they will be disappointed in you, or feel you don't love them because you don't want to spend your holiday with them. It is important to distinguish between your feelings and those you may be imagining are someone else's. You can't know how someone else feels, they are different from you, you can only know how you imagine they will feel.

Now review what you have learned and what you need to work with at this time.

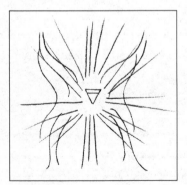

Archangel Uriel

As Archangel of the North and representing the element of earth, Uriel is very connected to the earth and base chakra as well as the solar plexus. He has a very determined, practical energy, which you'll be experiencing shortly. He is reputedly the angel who warned Noah of the impending flood and he helps with all mystical predictions. He will give you practical solutions and creative insight into all situations.

Clearing the Solar Plexus with Archangel Uriel

This is a very general exercise for you to adapt to your own needs as they change over time. If you have already written down the specifics of which areas you have chosen to work with on this occasion, it will help to remind yourself when you are in meditation. It will be easier than trying to remember it all.

As with the other exercises, practice in noticing what you notice will help you become more familiar with how you receive information from your higher self and the angels.

By now you are experienced at going into and out of meditations and I am sure you reach the fifth dimension very quickly by using your anchors. In this exercise I want you to put down your roots and open your chakras, but before going to the fourth and fifth dimensions, notice the colour, spin, of your solar plexus chakra at the third dimension. We live in the third dimension and although the clearing may be done at higher levels, it's in the third dimension that we need to notice the current state of the chakra and later any changes. If you wish, you could come out of the meditation and write a few notes in your journal or draw a picture of your chakra, before going back into the meditation. Then we will go to the other dimensions to do the work and stop again on the way back to notice the results.

As you become more experienced at going into and out of meditations at any point to make your notes, you gain the ability to get more information from your angels and unconscious, which will assist you in the future. This also starts to develop skills in automatic writing. Start to get used to coming back to a light trance where you can write your notes and going back in to where you left off.

If you are going to tape this meditation, please read it all the way through before making your tape, and remember to leave enough time between questions for you to get your answers. Be aware you can add questions of your own. Don't forget you can turn your tape off whilst writing.

So, begin to focus on your breathing, in and out, in and out and notice yourself getting more and more relaxed. When you are ready breathe down your roots, deep into the earth and as you breathe in open your chakras and protect yourself by pressing your thumb and first finger together.

Begin to focus your attention on your solar plexus. What sort of colour or colours does it contain, what shades of yellow, gold, brown, are those colours bright or dull? Is there a smell associated with this chakra, are you sensing any shapes within it? Which direction does it spin in? Notice which way it spins; is it fast, slow, sluggish? Is it round, or perhaps, oval? Just notice; let go of judgement, there is no right or wrong, it just is. Allow yourself to experience the energy in this chakra. Can you see or sense any blockages in the chakra. If so, what does it look like, what kind of form does it take, is it solid, is it sticky? What issue or issues are these blockages representing. What is it, what does it represent in your life? Perhaps you can talk to it; ask what it is, what does it need from you to help it, to give it permission to stop blocking you, what is its positive intention for you? It will have one, can it tell you what it is? Get as much information from your chakra as you can.

Come in and out to write your notes as necessary for you. Remember to just focus on your breathing to go back into the exercise after writing your notes.

This will probably take about 5 – 10 minutes

When you are ready and have learnt as much as you can for your highest good from the chakra, take yourself up to the fifth dimension to the space in which you meet your guardian angel by pressing your thumb and second and third fingers together.

Ask your guardian angel if they have any more information for you, perhaps you have not been too sure which angel is best placed to help you, ask your guardian angel right now. Then with your guardian angel invoke Archangel Uriel by repeating his name three times (*or in future medita-tions, invoke any other angel you wish to work with*). Notice if you are taken on a journey and if so what type of journey, to another temple, or where, what's the journey like, where do you go, who do you see or sense? When you arrive – or perhaps Uriel comes directly to you – notice the quality of the energy around you change. What do you see or sense or feel.

What do you notice about this energy? How is it making you feel, what do you see, sense, smell, taste in relation to this angel? If you are not sure which it is, don't worry, just be aware of what you are aware of.

Speak to Archangel Uriel.

(If you are taping this then leave 5 minutes)

If you already know what needs to be done then ask the angel to do it for you, to release old hurts, pains, misassumptions. Tell it what you need to let go of. If you are not aware what needs to be done then ask the angel to do whatever needs to be done for your highest good right now. What is Archangel Uriel *(or another angel you are working with)* doing? Is it using light and if so what colour light is it using to clear your solar plexus? Is it using its breath, if so what's the quality of the angel's breath? What does it feel like, cool, warm, cold, fresh, hot? Does the angel lead you to a warm pool of water, a shower, a crystal cave... How is Uriel *(or another angel)* clearing you?

Ask the angel what might be stopping you and what you need to do next to assist yourself in going forward in your life and your spiritual journey. Come out and make notes whenever you wish.

Leave another 5 – 10 minutes for this.

When the angel and yourself have done whatever needs to be done for now for your highest good, thank the angel and your guardian angel and begin to prepare yourself to come back through the dimensions to the third dimension fully open and protected. Before returning, notice your solar plexus chakra. What does it look like now, what changes have occurred to this chakra with this exercise? Just notice, let go of all judgement and know that what needed to be done has been done, and that the results will come just when the time is right for you.

When you have noticed the changes in your third chakra, reinforce your protection and breathing out, begin to let go of the fifth dimension by letting go of your thumb and fourth finger, let go of the fourth dimension by letting go of your thumb and second finger, protect and close yourself down, breathing up your roots and let go of your thumb and first finger. Gently wiggling your fingers and toes, come back into the room.

Now write and draw your experiences.

What have your learned from this experience?
What are you going to do differently now?
How have you progressed?
What is your next step on this journey?

Complete your records in your journal.

There are many issues and memories stored in the solar plexus. You can do this exercise as many times as you like. You'll always find new things or go to a deeper level of understanding in the main issues. Because this chakra is so important there are many other angels you can work with. You can see their various specialties below. If you are not sure, just ask for whichever angel you need most right now. Each time you do the exercise you can swap and change the angels and the areas you are working on.

Michael	The courage to be honest with yourself and others. (see chapter 9)
Uriel	Determination – the divine use of personal will not the stubborn will.
Phuel	Emotional tranquillity and stability. (Ask Phuel, or any of the water angels, to come whilst you are in the morning shower washing away any negativity from your aura and leaving you feeling calm and stable for the day ahead).
Micah	Letting go of indecision and addictions.
Fortunata	Good fortune and abundance – you attract into your life how much you feel you deserve so this is linked very much to self-worth.
Ramaela	Noticing the Joy in your life – connecting you to your eternal self which lives in Joy.

There are many levels and you can go round and around as many times as you wish, clearing and healing and making your life better.

Ramaela

After completing the above exercise you are going to allow yourself some indulgence. It is time to be good to yourself. The whole book is, in fact, about giving time to yourself, but here we are going to bring some joy and laughter into your life because laughter is a great tonic. When we laugh we release happy endorphins into our bodies and we feel lighter and

happier. So we shall be asking Ramaela to come and remind you of the joy you have in your life now and to help you notice it on a day-to-day basis.

Inviting Joy into your Life

Joy, like happiness, is not something that can be acquired. It's not, "I will be joyful when I go to that party", or "I will be happy when I get that promotion, new house," etc. Joy and happiness are already in our life but we don't necessarily notice. To feel joy or happiness is a spontaneous thing. It also comes in different guises. It shows itself in our body, in how we feel, not just in our thoughts.

As you read the next four paragraphs, notice what's happening in your body and what feelings come up. It may be that just a single sentence brings about a slight change or feeling. These are little subtle changes in your body. A rush of adrenaline would be a major one; these are similar but more subtle.

Stop and notice how your body is feeling right now. Is it relaxed, tense, tired? just notice. How are you sitting, are you slumped, are you upright, where are your shoulders?

Remember a sad occasion – how do you feel now, how is your body, how are you sitting, where are your shoulders?

Smile and notice how that changes the feelings in your body.

You are driving down a road and can see the sunshine on the autumn leaves – notice how it makes you feel. What do you normally do – do you appreciate the sheer joy of the experience or do you rush through the forest on your way somewhere, cutting up the car in front, inciting more aggressive driving, getting angry and stressed and maybe getting to your destination one or two minutes earlier.

Your baby smiles up at you, how do you feel? Can you take a moment to feel the joy and happiness that gives you, or do you rush to get the next feed ready?

Your husband comes home with a bunch of flowers. How do you feel, do you notice the shy, maybe embarrassed, loving smile in his eye behind the gruff thrusting hand saying "these are for you". Do you allow yourself to experience the love and the joy you feel at this unexpected gesture, or do you worry about getting them in water before the dinner burns, or wonder what's he feeling guilty about? This is your choice.

You have won £10 million on the lottery. How do you feel (not think – we think we would be happy if we won the lottery, whooping with joy, no doubt). Say to yourself, "I HAVE WON £10MILLION ON THE LOTTERY". How do you feel in your body? What's coming into your mind, what are you noticing, what are you unconsciously choosing to feel? Perhaps you feel light and free of financial worries, or do you feel the weight of responsibility for all that cash? Whatever you feel is OK just notice.

If you say things in the positive and you can notice what you feel in your body, you need never be indecisive again. Your body and your chakras are your direct connection to universal energy, the angels and your unconscious mind. You can always find out what's right for you. Ask Archangel Micah to help you with this. If there is no feeling response in your body then perhaps the time is not right to make a decision just yet, so let it go and be confident that you'll know when the time is right.

Connecting to Archangel Ramaela

For this, because you will want to invite Ramaela into your life on many and varied occasions, I suggest you use a simple invocation.

Close your eyes and focus on your breathing, so you are in a relaxed space, then just simply say her name three times. I usually say "Archangel Ramaela, angel of joy, Ramaela angel of laughter, I ask that you be present in my life. Ramaela, show me the joy that is here and to allow me to connect more closely to it. Bring me more joy and laughter into my life. Wrap me in your wings of laughter and joy so I might notice how much more there is in my life than I usually appreciate. So let it be".

Then notice how much better you feel. Notice all the little things that make you smile and laugh through your day and make notes of them in your journal in the evening.

CHAPTER 8

Chamuel

The Heart Chakra (four)

The heart chakra is the fourth chakra. It resides in the middle of our chest in the heart region. It is the chakra that acts as the gateway between the three lower chakras that focus on our physical being in this world and the three upper chakras that are related to our spiritual growth. It is where our divine essence of love is expressed in our human physical life.

In the heart chakra we are talking about pure unconditional love; the love of the universe, animals, God, our parents, partners and children. Love from a pure and unblocked heart chakra is completely unconditional. We put no boundaries, no conditions and no judgements on those we love. We don't control or manipulate, we love them, warts and all, we don't want to change them.

If our heart chakra is blocked – and most are – perhaps we have never experienced unconditional love. (Just look at the growing number of immune system diseases and growing cancer cases.) Perhaps love was only expressed to us if we were good, if we stopped crying, if we ate all our greens, if we got top marks at school, or won a competition. Perhaps, however much we tried, if we did not meet someone's expectations, expressions of love seemed to be withheld. I don't doubt our parents loved us. It is the expression of that love that has been missing, people are "too busy" therefore, the inner knowing and confidence that comes with it has been lost.

The heart chakra develops between the ages of 12 – 15 years old and many things can cause the heart chakra to close. Being rejected during growing up, the loss of a significant love in your life, parent, grandparent, pet. Any of these events can cause the chakra to close down. Below is a story which illustrates the kind of behaviour that can be expressed when someone closes their heart chakra to protect themselves from pain.

A person has a difficult relationship with a member of their family such as a father or mother as a teenager. They seem unable to get along. The parent is usually trying to control the child, who is in the process of trying to express themselves, and trying to gain recognition and acceptance of their own worth from the parent. The child really admires the parent and loves them but if their family has not been one for expressing love and affection openly, they can feel very unloved. The parent and child are always arguing they really can't get on. (This to most people will sound familiar and is a normal part of growth and individuation and in most circumstances is just a stage of development. But if this stage is interrupted and the relationship not reconciled it can lead to a very blocked heart chakra).

Unfortunately the parent suddenly dies, divorces, goes away to work, or in some other way ceases to be there for the child. How can the child express the love for the parent that they have suppressed and not felt or expressed for so long? How can they acknowledge how vulnerable they feel? They are not allowed to display emotion because that is the family rule. The child remembers all the rows and protects itself and feels the parent did not love them anyway. Now there are no rows, now life is easier, now they can be themselves without being judged. They have closed their heart to protect themselves from the pain of loss and their own sense of vulnerability.

Such people often go on to be critical and difficult to please, holding grudges for years. Often disliking many people and positively hating, and wanting revenge on those who they feel have let them down whilst at the same time seeing others as being able to do no wrong and placing them on a pedestal. If this person should fall off the pedestal, then rather than feel pain or let down, that person is immediately on the hated list.

People like this hold grudges for years and years and their anger and hatred eat away at them. They see rejection everywhere and usually withdraw before they can be rejected or more often, they never get into a position where they can be rejected. They have many layers of defences all around their hearts. These layers may have been valuable once in protecting the child from pain but now they rule the person's life, defending against imagined slights.

With a fully open, unblocked heart chakra, you experience the full expression of unconditional love. It is when we find a sense of compassion for ourselves that we finally fully open our heart chakra.

Our heart chakra is where love, compassion and the sense of touch reside. It is from where our sense of peace radiates when we are at peace with our world and ourselves.

If our hearts stop beating, we die. It beats automatically and it was always thought that we could not influence our hearts. When in panic our hearts beat faster, when afraid our hearts beat faster, our heart beats automatically, but in fact we can influence it. We can slow the pace of our heartbeat by simply focusing on our breathing, slowing down and noticing how this short meditation can make a difference. When working with the heart chakra people have different experiences but many people see colours ranging from pale rose pink through to deep magenta and or pale greens through to vibrant emerald greens, or sometimes both.

A Breathing Meditation

Just for a moment, notice your pulse and then begin to focus on your breathing, slow it right down, take in a breath to the count of four, breathe out to the count of four, expel all the air from your lungs, rest for the count of two, and breathe in to the count of six, breathe out to the count of six, and rest for the count of two. Breathe in to the count of eight, and breathe out to the count of eight, rest for the count of two, and relax into a natural rhythm.

Notice how much more relaxed and peaceful you feel, notice how the world seems softer and gentler. Notice the part of yourself that has gently begun to feel a deep sense of peace and acceptance. (You can do this anytime any place and just notice how your pulse has slowed.)

Heart Chakra

Location	Centre of chest
Colour	Green (sometimes with pink)
Developmental Age	12 – 15 years old
Sense	Touch
Glands / organs	Thymus, heart, circulatory system, arms, hands, lungs.

Concerns	Compassion, unconditional love, vulnerability, tenderness, detachment, hurt, bitterness, courage, passion, forgiveness.
Out of Balance	Inability to give or receive love. Expectations of others, inability to love (or to accept) yourself.
Body symptoms	Heart and vascular disease, diseases of the immune system (allergies, cancer, AIDS, ME).
Qualities / Lessons	Divine / unconditional love. Forgiveness, compassion, balance, understanding, group consciousness, oneness with life, acceptance, peace, openness, harmony contentment.
Negative qualities	Repression of love, emotional instability, out of balance.
Positive qualities growth, healing	Unconditional love, acceptance, inner harmony hope,
Soul Issue	To give and receive love without condition. To find strength in vulnerability.
Element	Air
Gems & Minerals	Emerald, green and pink tourmaline, malachite, green jade, green aventurine, chrysoprase, kunzite, rose quartz, ruby.
Associated Angels	Archangel Chamuel, Archangel Raphael, all Angels of Healing, Phuel, Archangel Jophiel.
Associated Oils	Benzoine, bergamot, cinnamon, clove, elemi, geranium, grapefruit, immortelle, lavender, lime, linden blossom, mandarin, neroli, palmarosa, rose, sandalwood.

The Heart

Our physical heart controls our blood circulatory system, without our physical heart we can't live and without a well-balanced and open-heart chakra we can't experience our true loving potential.

Fear is our biggest block around the heart chakra. Fear of loss. Fear of losing those we love. Fear of loving and opening ourselves to the possibility of loss. Even fear of feeling love because of the lack of it that comes to our attention. Fear of being manipulated, such as "I will love you if..." fear of not being good enough, fear of being rejected by our families, partners, children, colleagues, the world. Fear of what others think and how they might judge us. Fear of not being accepted.

No one has the right to judge another and yet we seem to live in a very judgemental world. But however hard we might try, we do judge others, it is almost a habit. It is part of being human, something that is ingrained in our society and culture. But we are hardest on ourselves. We judge ourselves remorselessly. "I'm not good enough, I must try harder, if they can do it, why can't I. I want to be... I will be happy when ..."

The only way we can ever begin to open the heart chakra and begin to receive and give unconditional love is to accept ourselves as we are. This does not mean you are selling out and you are going to stop striving for progress, in fact, it means exactly the opposite. Accepting where you are now gives us the ability to grow and develop, a launch pad of solid ground rather than constantly shifting sands. We don't need to be complacent or arrogant and say, "We have done it all we don't need to change", it's just that where we are now is fine and we are fine. Allowing some compassion for ourselves and indulging ourselves just as we would a child who has tried to stand up and walk, fallen over, and reverted to crawling for a while before trying to stand up again. When doing any self-development work such as the exercises in this book, we need to learn to walk before we can run, we need to be OK with where we are now.

"Your outer journey may contain a million steps; your inner journey has only one: the step you are taking right now. As you become more deeply aware of this one step, you realise that it already contains within itself all the other steps as well as the destination..."
Eckhart Tolle, *The Power of Now*

Breathing in Peace Meditation

Another exercise which is very good for opening the heart chakra is to imagine yourself breathing in peace and love down through your head and transforming your own anger, resentments, self-judgements into unconditional love for yourself or someone with whom you might be having a difficult relationship.

Imagine your heart chakra as a small flower bud. Imagine the energy coming down through your head and your shoulders down to your heart and, as you breathe out, the flower petals gently begin to open. The flower might be pink and or green, whatever colour is right for you. As you breathe out you allow your heart to fill with the unconditional love of the universe and to send it to yourself or to another.

Notice how big the petals are, notice whether it is fully open; even just a single movement of a single petal shows progress. Notice how this makes you feel. You can do this exercise as much as you like, you will see the progress you make with your heart chakra opening by how open the flower becomes. You can also see how you relate to various people. Notice how far your petals open when you think of different people. This exercise can help change your relationships with people, as in the story below.

Example

I did this many years ago when I was working in marketing. The firm I worked for merged and I had applied for the job of national marketing manager of one of the divisions. I really wanted this job and felt I was ready for the responsibility. Unfortunately the firm we had merged with did not and decided to put in one of their own managers and made me the assistant manager. I was not a happy bunny. It was not my new boss's fault that she was rated more highly than me or that she got the job rather than me, but that did not stop the feelings of anger, resentfulness, and jealousy that I felt for her. Those feelings were my problem not hers, but that did not make me easy to work with.

I did not like feeling that way, these feelings were new to me, I had not been aware I could feel that way, because in my family I had to be nice and good and nice girls did not get angry. I had shut off all these types of feelings from myself many years earlier. I wondered what I could do, so I did the exercise we did earlier, visualising a flower in my heart chakra and bringing down unconditional love to transform my negative energies into positive unconditional love to send to my boss.

Boy was it hard. Every day, on the way to work, and especially on the way home, I would sit on the underground/subway and imagine breathing in the unconditional love of the universe and letting it transform all my negative emotions towards my boss and breathing out unconditional love for her. This went on for months and slowly but surely my relationship with her changed. We worked together and became a really good team. Even though our lives have now taken us in different directions and to different parts of the world, we are still really good friends.

One day whilst doing the exercise, I experienced an overpowering feeling of love for everyone, completely unconditional love for everyone and everything around me, (which on the London Underground in the rush hour is not easy). I realised my heart chakra, which I had always seen as a small rose and which I thought had been fully open, had only been open a fraction because suddenly it turned into a huge rose that was in full bloom. I felt the presence of a huge loving energy and saw a mass of bright pink light. I said to myself, "what's this?" A little voice inside my heart said, "I'm Archangel Chamuel, I have watched you practice this exercise and seen your dedication in trying to break down your barriers to love. So I am here to help you feel what unconditional love really feels like. Absorb this, recognise it as your own true self and know that it will develop more and more as your life goes on. Love is everything, don't be afraid."

As you can imagine I was over-awed, after all I was sitting on the London underground and not even particularly trying either. (That is the secret – not trying too hard). The love I felt brought tears to my eyes because I had never felt anything like it before. Old habits die hard because almost before I was aware, my defences came in and I closed down to these feelings, because there was no way I could not allow myself to cry in public (old family rule).

It has taken many more years of practice and accepting where I am on my journey to begin to feel even a fraction of what I felt on the underground that day. But I have experienced the full potential of my life and of universal love and I am grateful.

The more we love, accept and respect ourselves and those around us, just as we are, the more others will follow our example and love, accept and respect us and everyone else, and this is where Archangel Chamuel comes in.

What Makes your Heart Sing?

Ask yourself the following questions:

What makes your heart sing?

Is there something or someone you would like to let go of or release?

Can you express your love and your feelings without fearing how it will be received?

Do you judge yourself and others?

What do you expect from those you love?

Bring up an image to mind of someone you don't like. Can you find something to like about them?

In what situations do you feel compassion?

Can you feel compassion for yourself?

Can you feel compassion for those you love?

Do you tend to think negatively?

Are you pessimistic?

Do you hold grudges?

Do you see some people as all good and others as all bad?

Are you difficult to please?

Are you afraid of loving and being loved?

Consider these questions and any more that come to mind. Write your answers in your journal, draw the feelings that are brought up in you and see what you learn about yourself.

Archangel Chamuel

Archangel Chamuel connects us to the unconditional love of the universe and assists us in identifying and lowering the proactive mechanisms we have built up through the course of our lives to protect our true vulnerable selves from the hurts and (most probably unintentional) rejections of our pasts.

I believe unconditional love develops constantly over our lives, gradually opening more and more as we become more aware of our own inner selves, our defences, accepting ourselves and others exactly where we are now unconditionally on our journey rather than constantly trying to rush to the end of it.

Chamuel will come into your life and very gently open your heart to yourself and to others. In this chapter's exercise and visualisation we will go on a journey to meet Archangel Chamuel. You should be very good at doing this by now. Then we will allow Chamuel and any other angels who may wish to lend us a hand to come and help identify the barriers you place around yourself and how you may begin to let them down, as and when you wish to. These barriers have been built for a purpose and they have served you faithfully, protecting you from fear, love, loss, pain, but now you will be able to choose when to use them, and when not to. This exercise will help you identify and lower your defences to allow you to let more love into your life.

Connecting to Archangel Chamuel

Make yourself comfortable, turn off the phone. If you wish to light a candle please make sure it is in a safe position. You can use any of the oils or crystals mentioned in the table at the beginning of this chapter. For this I usually have rose quartz and two sticks of incense, English rose and sandalwood as I particularly like this combination for the heart chakra. Put on some soft music and if you are going to put the visualisation on tape then please read it through and ensure you leave enough blank space on the tape to be able to do the work. I will give indications as we go through. Have your journal to hand to record your experiences. Depending upon how often you have practiced earlier exercises, you may go in and out of the exercise in your own time to record your experiences. Take time when you feel it is appropriate.

So relax and begin to focus on your breathing, in and out, in and out, breathing in peace and love and breathing out all negativity. Take yourself up through the dimensions quickly and easily, using your anchors; you are very practiced by now.

As you go higher and higher you become more and more relaxed and you feel your guardian angel's energy around you. You are already familiar with the loving energy of your guardian angel and other angels but this time you are asking to be taken to the temple of Archangel Chaumel to get assistance with identifying your barriers and defences to love and to find out what you need to do to be able to let those barriers down as and when you wish and to let you experience more love in your life.

So feel the energy and allow your guardian angel's wings to surround and support you as you float gently across the universe to the temple of Archangel Chaumel. Remember that whatever you experience is just right for you and some of you may find that you are instantly transported to Chamuel's temple, others may feel Chamuel's presence in their own space. Whatever you experience is just right for you at this time, another time when you do the exercise you may experience something completely different and that will be just right for you as well.

What does Chamuel feel like to you, how do you experience this energy, is it male or female for you? What colours do you experience with this angel, what smells are present? Is this angel large or small, is it enveloping you or standing back, what is this energy, what does Chamuel feel like to you? How will you recognise this energy again? Ask Chamuel whatever questions you wish about how the barriers to love were formed. Listen to Chamuel's reply. What does this angel have to say about these barriers, what was their purpose, how did they protect you, were the rejections real or imaginary?

You may remember certain events in your early life or you may not. You may get an impression of something but not be able to remember the occasion. Whatever you get is just right for you, right now. So listen, sense, see what Chamuel has to tell you. Come out and make notes whenever you wish because you can go back in and pick up from wherever you like.

(If taping leave 3 - 5 minutes here. Remember to turn off your tape when you come out to write your notes.)

Now you have some sense of how and why these barriers were formed. I want you to respect these barriers and thank these barriers for protecting you for so long.

(If taping leave 30 seconds)

Now imagine a bright light like a torch probing through your body, looking for these barriers around your heart. What do they look like, what are they made of, how many of them are there, are they like a Russian doll with many other smaller ones all inside? What are your barriers like? Are they solid, thick, like an impenetrable safe? What are they made of, what do they smell like, how do they feel, hard, solid, sticky, gluey, prickly, impenetrable, railings you can see though? Are there more forming? Can you see past your barriers, can you see, sense or feel what's at the centre of your heart? What are you protecting so fiercely. What is it, what might it need? Spend some time noticing your barriers and what they are protecting. If you can't get to the middle of them right now that's fine. This is a gentle process you can come back to and do over again on other occasions in the future.

(If taping leave 5 minutes on tape)

Now as you begin to know what's being protected, ask what this part of you needs and how these barriers might be able to help it develop. What do you need to do to be able to lower the barriers one by one when you wish, when it is your choice, when it is the choice of the part of you inside the heart? What do you need to be able to let go of some of the barriers.

(If taping leave 3 minutes on tape)

What's the fear that prevents you and what does that fearful part need from you or from Archangel Chamuel to allow you to experience gently opening your heart chakra to unconditional love at your choosing.

(If taping leave 3 minutes on tape)

Then gently ask yourself and Archangel Chaumel if there's anything else that needs to be done or anything else you need to know before the healing can take place. You and Archangel Chamuel can begin to let the barriers down one by one and allow in complete unconditional love for yourself and others. Do you feel you can love some people unconditionally but not others? Do you feel you can love the world but not the individual? Do you feel you can love everyone except yourself? Ask what you need to do to be able to accept and love yourself right now ... listen to your heart, listen to Archangel Chamuel. Can you do what needs to be done for you, can you accept yourself right now? If not what could you do as the next step... the first step was choosing to buy this book, the next has been all the other exercises, the latest is doing this exercise, so what's the next step that you need to take for you?

(If taping leave a minute or two)

Now imagine a light coming down through your head and filling your body, encompassing your whole self inside and out. Or do whatever is right for you and whatever you need to be able to let your barriers go. This light may be of any colour, white, pink, green, or any other color you need most now in your life. Feel the light and the color come down. Feel it permeate your being, see it begin to dissolve those barriers one by one, just as much as feels right for you right now. Know that you can put them back again when necessary, know that you can let them gently dissolve in the light to whatever level of protection, or not, you need right now in your life.

You are opening to the power of the unconditional love of the universe that is yours by right by Divine law. Let the love flow over you, dissolving those barriers, touching your inner self and igniting the flame of unconditional love in your heart. Expanding it out through your barriers, out into your aura, out into the room, the house, the street, the neighbourhood, the country, the world, the universe. Breathe that love in and out.

How does that feel, in every sinew of your body?

(If taping leave a minute or two)

Now it is time to thank Archangel Chamuel and your inner self for the insights and experiences you have received. Know that you can return to this place at any time in the future to continue this work, dismantling those barriers, checking in on your inner self. Know you have choice. You can let go fear and re-experience this wonder whenever you wish in the future. Thank your barriers for the protection they have given you, respect the help they have given you in your life when it was necessary, but affirm that now you are going to choose when to use these barriers and when not. Let Archangel Chamuel go, fading gently into the distance.

Allow yourself to return to the arms of your guardian angel and slowly return to the room, letting go of your anchors and wiggling your fingers and toes. Have a drink of water to ground yourself back in the present.

Remember to capture your experiences in your journal in whichever way is right for you and to reflect on what you have learned and what you intend to do differently now.

CHAPTER 9

Gabriel, Michael and Zadkiel

"In the beginning was the Word and the Word was with God..." These are the opening words of St John's gospel. Some scientists are beginning to believe that sound is the underlying pattern of the universe. Sound is a vibration, an invisible energy and energy creates form. As we send out energy in the form of sound, change happens.

Most of you will have heard of daily affirmations, saying something out loud in the positive many times, such as "I am happy" creates feelings of happiness within you. "I am a divine being just like everybody else", lets go of feeling not good enough without risking inflating a false ego.

Listening is a great skill, being able to hear what people are saying, what they are really saying, what they mean. Most of us speak in riddles and misunderstand most of what is said to us by others. We assume people understand what we mean even if we don't put it into so many words. This usually works within our own family group because everyone is used to it and we unconsciously understand the family rules, but with people outside the family it is more open to misunderstanding, as they don't know the unwritten rules of the family and therefore will use their own unwritten rules to interpret what you say. They will make their own assumptions, as you do, and may completely misunderstand what you meant, and you may misunderstand the meaning of what they say too.

In this chapter we will be working with Archangel Gabriel, the angel of communication, because everything we do is some form of communication, with ourselves or with others. We will also work with Archangel Michael, the angel of truth, courage and protection, who can give you the courage to be honest with yourself and can, with his golden sword, cut the cords that bind you to the past. This may be people, situations, feelings, or anything that you no longer need.

With Archangel Zadkiel we will be letting go of any past life vows that may be holding you back in your current life. Vows and promises are spoken, so this comes from the throat chakra. Vows or promises are made at various stages in our soul's development and if we don't release ourselves from these vows and promises then we are not able to move on with our current journey as easily as we could. How often do you notice that you intend to say something but it gets stuck in your throat?

The upper chakras work on a soul/spiritual level while the lower ones work on the physical level. They must all be in balance to work efficiently. The upper ones can't develop any faster than the lower ones let go of their issues.

So far we have been working with the chakras individually but they are in fact connected and work in pairs. The pairs relate like this:

Crown	Base
Third Eye	Sacrum
Heart	(joins the upper and lower the psychical to the spiritual)
Throat	Solar Plexus

Therefore you can work with any angel from the relating chakra as well.

As we clear and go up through the chakras, you'll be connecting to the higher soul elements of your life. The healing exercise from Chapter 3 will automatically clear your chakras but we will also do a quick exercise in this chapter to clear and balance all the chakras. I will also give you guidelines on toning to specifically help you clear your throat chakra. Like everything else, the more you do these exercises, the more you'll open up to the full potential of your life.

As we progress through the higher chakras, you may notice how your intuitive skills are developing. You are becoming more self aware and able to trust and follow your gut reactions. You may also notice your clairaudient, clairsentient and clairvoyant skills start to emerge. The more you clear your chakras, both lower and higher, the more these abilities will develop naturally of their own accord.

But first let me tell you a little about the angels we are working with in this section.

Archangel Gabriel

There are many stories of Gabriel. He is the angel who brought the message to Joseph and the Virgin Mary announcing the birth of Jesus. He is the angel who dictated the Koran to Mohammed. He was reputedly the voice of Joan of Arc. Gabriel will also connect you with your soul's purpose and your destiny when the time is right.

Gabriel is the archangel of communication. He is one of the four great archangels. He is the angel of the west, and he represents the element of water.

Many years ago when I first read about Archangel Gabriel being the angel of communication, the thought of asking him for help when communicating seemed rather far-fetched.

At the time I was working for a subsidiary of a large organisation when a new marketing director was appointed. We were as different as chalk and cheese and it quickly became apparent that it would not be easy to work together. I was called to see him one Monday morning and I fully expected to have to resign or get fired, so I asked Gabriel to help me communicate my views both to myself (because I was not sure what I wanted or how to handle the situation) and to him, so as to bring about a solution for the highest good of all concerned. Then I went in. We started talking about the difficulties and issues between the way we worked, the direction he wanted to take the department and where I wanted to go with my career. Within half an hour a very different solution was found. I was promoted to another department. Not a solution I would have dared think of let alone ask for.

At work I was plagued with having too many meetings to attend, all of which went on much too long, talking about nothing and not coming to any conclusions. So I started asking Gabriel to ensure the meeting went as quickly and smoothly as possible and that workable conclusions resulted for the highest good of all concerned. I said this little prayer on my way to every meeting. It never failed. Things did not always go my way but whatever ensued was something I could live with and was workable for all concerned. Increasingly I seemed to get my points across much better than I ever had before and, as a result more and more did start to go my way. It works – try it.

It works with children too. My daughter had a problem at school that had been going on for quite some time and I could not get to the bottom of it. She seemed insecure and kept being ill and wanting to stay at home. I asked for help and within 24 hours I discovered what had been troubling her and was able to sort it out and she returned to the happy confident child she had always been.

Archangel Michael

Archangel Michael is one of the four mighty archangels. He brings courage, truth and protection. He sits in the south and represents the element of fire. He is said to be chief of the order of Virtues as well as chief of all the archangels. Michael ranks as the mightiest of angels in Jewish, Christian and Islamic religions. He is often referred to as the prince of light. He is the warrior angel. He is believed to be the angel of Mons, who appeared over the battlefield during the First World War, whose appearance changed the tide of the war.

Michael is often prevalent in peoples' lives and can sometimes be the first angel after your guardian angel to makes his presence felt. When Michael is around you often feel a great deal of heat because he represents the element of fire. I always know it's him because I get so very hot. I find he comes to help when I am healing, especially if my client needs to let go of things from the past.

Throat Chakra (Five)

Location	Throat
Colour	Blue – turquoise / aquamarine / sky blue / bright blue.
Developmental Age	15 – 21 years old
Sense	Hearing
Glands / organs	Thyroid, parathyroid, hypothalamus, throat, mouth.
Concerns	Self-expression, trust, freedom, speaking your truth.
Out of Balance	Incessant chattering, or feeling choked off, inability to speak up and speak out, keeping quiet.
Body symptoms	Problems of the thyroid, sore throat, tonsillitis, tinnitus, hearing difficulties.
Qualities / Lessons	Power of the spoken word, true communication, creative expression in speech, writing and the arts, integration, peace, truth, knowledge, wisdom, loyalty, honesty, reliability, gentleness, kindness.
Negative qualities	Communication and or speech problems, ignorance, knowledge used unwisely, inability to act, lack of discernment, depression.
Positive qualities	Self-expression, will, creative expression, joy, honesty, spontaneity
Soul Issue	To feel free to speak honestly and openly. To trust the soul to speak its truth
Element	Ether
Gems & Minerals	Aquamarine, azurite, blue lace agate, chrysocolla, celestite, kyanite, lapis lazuli, sodalite, blue topaz, turquoise.
Associated Angels	Archangel Michael, Archangel Gabriel, Zadkiel
Associated Oils	Black pepper, blue chamomile, cajeput, cypress, elemi, eucalyptus, myrrh, palmarosa, ravensara, rosemary, sage, yarrow.

It is through the throat that we express ourselves. We make sounds, words, songs and tunes. We first cry to attract the attention of our parents or carers. Although we communicate in many different ways, including body language and tone of voice, and although our words only make up 7 per cent of our total communication with others, it's a very important 7 per cent! How we speak, what we say, how we say it, how it is received and interpreted by others, all influence how we live our lives. When you change your manner of speech the reactions of others change towards you.

The throat chakra includes our ears, our listening skills. If we have a clear and well-functioning throat chakra, we leave indecisiveness behind because we not only fully understand ourselves, we can know and speak up about our own truth, we are honest and we live with integrity.

Obviously we all have our own thoughts and feelings about what's true for us and we have our own morality and integrity that is personal as well as culturally based. This is always changing as we move through our lives, as we learn and develop more, as our views change. It is important to have compassion for your younger self who didn't know as much then as you know now, even if it was only an hour ago when you were making decisions and taking actions that you might not do now. Actions we take now that we might not have taken before, either because someone else told us "no" or we were fearful of what others might think. These are all issues that we have been dealing with and will continue to deal with as we change and progress through our lives.

It takes courage to admit that we could have been wrong, that maybe we should not have acted in a certain way, or done something. We all have things in our past that we wish we had not done, that we are not proud of. This is our learning. Having compassion for ourselves, forgiving ourselves and others, listening to that still quiet voice within ourselves, the voice of our soul, and finding the courage to hear, speak and act our truth and just as importantly hear the truth of others – all without judgement.

Challenges in the Throat Chakra

Questions you can ask yourself to see if you have any blockages in your throat chakra.

If I say what I think, will people accept me?

If I ask for what I want and need, will I be thought of as selfish?

I can't say what I feel to that person because they might be hurt.

What will my boss think if I ask for a pay rise?

Are there areas in your life that you want to leave behind?

Has someone passed over suddenly and you did not get a chance to say how you felt?

Do you have trouble expressing yourself?

Do you have trouble being heard? Do people not understand you?

Do you avoid confrontation?

Do you often think of what you could have said in a situation but didn't at the time?

Do you feel resentful or angry towards anyone in your past or present?

Are you still angry or hurt over a past relationship or job?

Do you suffer from throat problems such as losing your voice, if so what might be a common link between those occasions?

Spend some time answering these questions in your journal and pick on something you would like to work on next. Invoke Archangel Gabriel and Archangel Michael by repeating their names three times to help you find the courage to look deep into your heart and unconscious to find the honest answers to the questions above and any others and to communicate them to your conscious mind.

I usually say something like,

"I ask archangel Michael, Michael of the south, Michael of the element of fire and Archangel Gabriel, Gabriel of the west, Gabriel of communication to be with me now, to give me the courage to communicate honestly with myself and to identify whatever I need to work on now for my highest good. So let it be."

Then I focus on my breathing and settle myself for a moment or two. I then begin the exercise, knowing I will identify whatever needs to be dealt with most right now at whichever level, for my highest good.

When you have identified what you need to let go of right now, you can go onto the next exercise where you'll go on a journey to meet Archangel Michael and Archangel Gabriel and work with them both to cut the cords that bind you to the past. You can also intend this to work across time to cut any cords that are binding you from past lifetimes as well.

Journey to Archangel Michael and Archangel Gabriel

Begin to focus on your breathing, breathing down your roots and breathing up the earth energy, up through your chakras, up to your crown, pressing your thumb and first finger together and feeling yourself fully protected and open.

Now pressing your thumb and second finger together, feel yourself on the island with your guide and your loved ones, with all your fourth dimensional chakras in place. Begin to feel yourself on that escalator going up to the crystal temple to meet your guardian angel with all your fifth dimensional chakras in place. As you press your thumb and third finger together, you find yourself with your guardian angel. Be aware that your guardian angel is going to take you across the universe to meet Archangel Michael, who will help you to cut the cords that bind you to people, places and emotions that are holding you back in this lifetime.

Feel your guardian angel's wings around you holding you safely warm and snug as he teleports you across the universe to a beautiful temple or space of your choosing. Feel and see lots of angels around you and as you enter they part and you see, sense and hear two angels before you. Know that these are Archangel Michael and Archangel Gabriel. Feel their presence. Spend time with each of them individually, feel their energies, notice the differences. What colours do they show, how do their separate energies feel to you, how do they feel when they come closer and combine? What do they look like? Notice Michael's golden sword feel his presence and that of Gabriel as you press your thumb and fourth finger together.

Feel the warmth of Archangel Michael's element of fire, the warrior angel, feel his courage and protection. He will help you. He will give you the courage to be honest and truthful with yourself. Feel Archangel Gabriel, know that he will help you know intuitively just what's right for you, he will give you the words you need to say, he will ensure it all flows smoothly. Now Archangel Michael and Gabriel are leading you to the centre of the temple, to a golden circle and as you stand within the circle, another golden circle appears in front of you, forming a figure eight, the symbol of eternity, so you are healing your karma across all directions of time, for yourself and all others concerned.

Know that you are going to be cutting away any emotions, resentments, anger or fears, anything or anybody who is holding you back in this lifetime. Ask the angels to bring forward to the other circle anyone whom you need to cut away from, or a representation of any emotion or feeling you need to cut away from, and know that whoever or whatever appears in the circle it is just right for you at this time. Trust your imagination, just trust what happens in your imagination. These people can be in life or in spirit.

Notice the healing circle of angels surrounding you encouraging you, notice Michael on your left and Gabriel to your right. Their wings outstretched totally surrounding you and this person or representation, and know you can say whatever you need to say to this person or emotion, allow it to all come out. Take your time; there will be no hurt to you or to anyone else while you are in the circle. Just feel the emotions and know that Gabriel is giving you permission to express yourself freely.

(If taping leave 5 – 10 minutes)

When you have said all there is to be said, allow yourself to be that person or emotion. Be that other person. What do they have to say right now? What was their positive intention in the situation? Continue this conversation for as long as it takes.

(If taping leave 5 minutes)

If necessary, ask Gabriel or Michael what they would have to say about this situation.

(If taping leave a minute or two)

Then, when everything that needs to be said and understood has been completed, ask to see the cords that are binding you to this person, situation or emotion or place, imagine these cords, feel and see these cords. What do they look like, just a jumble of cords or a single cord? Where do they go? What chakra do they connect to? What are they? How are they linked? What are they called – ungratefulness, anger, jealousy, grief... Whatever they are, just see Archangel Michael draw his sword and start to cut the cords at both ends, know that he is cutting these cords across all directions of time, letting go of any past life issues which may be connected to this person, place, and healing the wounds by placing his golden sword on each end. Feel the healing taking place until you are completely free, let go, let go, let go.

(If taping leave a few minutes)

Well done. If it is a person you no longer wish to have in your life, just imagine them getting smaller and smaller and fading away into the distance. If it is someone you wish to keep in your life, then imagine a single cord going from your heart chakra to their heart chakra, full of unconditional love. Feel the love flow between you and know you are sending healing to the other person, wherever they may be, whether they be in this realm or the next you are sending healing to them and in this process you are healing the past, the present and the future across all dimensions of time and space.

Then when you have finished, thank Archangel Michael and Archangel Gabriel for their help and allow your guardian angel to wrap you in its wings and, letting go of your thumb and fourth finger, allow yourself to be taken back across the universe to your guardian angels temple and letting go of your thumb and third finger and the fifth dimensional chakras, find yourself back in your garden with your guide and loved ones. Now let go of your thumb and second finger and all the fourth dimensional chakras and find yourself on the cliff, looking across at the island. Feel yourself fully protected and breathing out close yourself down, breath up your roots and let go of your thumb and first finger. Gently bring yourself back into the room by wriggling your fingers and toes and opening your eyes.

Well done.

Know that you can use this exercise as many times in the future as you wish. Sometimes it is good to go back into the same situation and see if you are still free because we can re-grow the cords, but each time there are less and less.

Now write and draw your impressions of Archangel Michael and Archangel Gabriel and your experiences of this exercise in your journal. What have you learned? What insights did you gain, especially of the other person involved? What where they trying to achieve for you?

Releasing Anger and Grieving

I have done this exercise many times and I remember the first time how it frightened me. My mother had died when I was only nine years old and I knew I needed to let her go. I was 45 and had never really grieved for her. It was very difficult and painful. What surprised me most was how much I hated her for dying. It was completely illogical but the feelings were very real and had been suppressed all my life. My defence had been to hate God instead.

When I had completed the exercise I thought I was a really bad person for hating her so much. I was amazed at the rage I felt but I did feel better. The rage was most probably all the suppressed emotions of my inner two year old – you know, "the terrible twos", never being allowed to do what I wanted or express my anger because "good girls don't". Then I started feeling guilty about it all. So there, unbeknown at that time, I was now growing a new cord of guilt. I also realised how much I had unconsciously turned that hate on myself because how can you hate your own mother whom you also love.

When I started to write and draw and do the exercise again and again I began to realise that I kept growing new cords, which were my guilt, shame and other emotions. I began to realise that I kept growing these cords back because although I consciously wanted to let go, unconsciously I was not ready yet, so as fast as I cut I grew them back. Slowly but surely I let go of my guilt, my shame at how I felt so angry at something that was nobody's fault and certainly not hers. I brought the angels into my life to support and help my inner child so that part of me could feel secure enough to let my mother go.

It took a few sessions but when I check in on my mum now we are connected across time by one cord of unconditional love. Since I did this exercise and let her go I have begun to get messages from her, I have begun to feel her presence around me. Until then she had not been able to get through because I had been protecting myself from all the emotions I had not been able to experience and let go of.

Unexpressed grief

After my mother's death my father told me not to cry because "big girls don't cry" and it would upset everyone else, especially my grandmother. I was sent to the country to stay with my aunt and was not allowed to go to the funeral.

I walked the hills with my aunt's dog but could not cry, let alone scream the terrible pain inside me. All I felt was that nothing could ever be the same again and the sun had no right to rise again. But none of the family would talk about anything so I had to keep it all in.

A few years ago I had an EFI photo taken which showed big red lines across my throat chakra and problems with my sinuses. The following month my faithful dog was dying and boy did it hurt. I was in pain again, another loss. I theoretically knew better but still found it really difficult to speak or cry about it. I knew I needed to and I knew it was also related to my mothers' death but however much I tried I could not get anything out. My throat was so bad I lost my voice. I kept working on my throat chakra, cleaning it, opening it, toning when I could, I did everything I could think of until one day, three days after my dog died, I started to scream. I screamed for two hours. I let out all the pain of the past in one go. A month later I had another aura photo done, which showed most of the blockages as having gone. I have virtually no sinus or throat trouble since and when I do I ask myself "what am I not expressing?"

Mantras

Another way of opening and clearing your chakras (especially the throat chakra) is saying a mantra out loud over and over again. There are many different mantras, one of the most famous being the sound "Om". You can say your name over and over with different intonations voices and notes, again this can be a very spiritual experience. Many years ago I was in a workshop where as a group we took it in turns to sing each person's name, as a mantra. It was a really amazing experience, there was not one person who was not deeply affected by the love that seemed to be created by this simple act and sound. You can use any phrase of great meaning to you as a mantra.

Many things can get stuck in our chakras and meridian energy system because they are all interrelated. Everything that happens, any undealt-with emotional issues, feelings, great or small can get blocked in the system and often get stuck in the throat chakra, especially if we have not expressed them. These blockages can be photographed with a special energy field illumination (EFI) camera, which shows all the blockages within the chakras and meridians. For more details see my website www.joylina.com.

Letting go of Past Life Vows with Archangel Zadkiel

Many people and many religions believe that we all have had many lifetimes before, that we incarnate into this physical world to experience life. It's through our bodies that we experience this life, not through our minds and our thoughts. We experience our world though the senses of our body. We can create a thought, which we manifest through seeing how we feel about that idea: is it a good one, will it work, does it feel right to us? Then we take action and do something, get it done, or whatever is needed and then it is manifested.

We have all had many other lifetimes and we have had different experiences in each of those lifetimes as well as this lifetime. This is why everyone is different. No one knows how another feels. We can have empathy, we may feel we understand if we have had similar experiences ourselves but we can't know how another feels because it is their feelings not ours. I know how I felt when my husband died and I can imagine how another woman might feel when she has lost her husband but I can't experience her feelings. I can only feel my own and imagine hers.

Everyone comes into this life with karma. This is a Hindu concept originating in India, which in essence means that the acts of our past lives will be influencing our lives today. Vows from previous lives can also affect our behaviour in this lifetime. Maybe others always need your help and you never get anything done for yourself, perhaps you took a vow to help others. Perhaps you seem to expect the world to owe you a living, or you don't think you should have to work, maybe you feel you should just think and contemplate the meaning of life. This could mean that you were a Buddhist monk who was brought food by others in return for prayers. Maybe you are not interested in sex because you took a vow of celibacy. Letting go of these past life vows can allow you to look differently at things in your life today and to bring abundance into your current life.

There are many angels you can call on for help in letting go of past life vows: Archangel Gabriel, Archangel Michael, Zadkiel, Micah, Zagzagel and your own guardian angel. This is the one I like because your guardian angel has been with you through all your lifetimes and knows all the vows of poverty, chastity, revenge that you may have taken. Remember, many people in your life now may be people you have had past lives with. People you instantly like, people you instantly dislike or fear.

Each vow or promise you have ever made, whether it be positive or negative, is in the keeping of an angel and by releasing these vows you'll be releasing yourself – and the angels – to be free to move on to other things. These vows will be released into the energy of Archangel Zadkiel's breath of the violet flame, to be transformed. It is not necessary to know what these vows are for the exercise to be effective but it can throw much light on your life to date if you can see what these vows are. From the ideas above you'll resonate with some and not others. You'll know at a deep level which ones apply to you.

You can do the exercise as many times as you wish and if the person you made the promise or vow to is with you in this lifetime you can combine it with going through an imaginary conversation with them as you did in the "Cutting the Cords that Bind You" exercise with Archangel Michael and Archangel Gabriel.

Visualisation to Release Vows

Sit back, relax, and prepare for a short exercise. Ensure you are open, protected and have reached the space where you meet your guardian angel. Then with your guardian angel ask Archangel Zadkiel to be with you. Experience the energy, notice what you notice, and ask him to help you let go of any vows or promises you have made in this lifetime and past lifetimes that are no longer necessary and that are holding you back from reaching your full potential.

These may be vows for revenge on another soul, vows of forgiveness, vows of poverty, chastity, silence, even vows of becoming very rich at whatever cost. They could be vows of priesthood/priestesshood, vows to gods and goddess of the past that you no longer need in this lifetime. You are asking to be set free of all vows that have no relevance to this current life and that are inhibiting you reaching your full spiritual potential right now.

See lots of angels coming towards you and one by one they let go of the vow they are holding in their hands. Watch as it floats off like a puff of smoke, up into the violet flame of Archangel Zadkiel's breath, to be transformed.

Stay with this process for as long as you feel you need. It is not necessary to know each of these vows, just know they were necessary at the time, whatever they were, positive or negative and that now you are being released to go on into your future with nothing holding you back. When you are ready, ask Archangel Zadkiel to wrap you in his violet breath and to cleanse and transform any negative energy in and around you into positive energy for you to use and share with others.

When you feel ready begin to come back into the room.

Inner Listening

Listening is a great skill. Being able to hear what people are saying, understanding what they really are saying, what they mean. Most of us speak in riddles and misunderstand most of what is said to us by others. We assume people understand what we mean even if we don't put it into so many words. This usually works within your own family group but not with outsiders. It is often a good idea to check out any assumptions we make but this is difficult because most of the time they are so subtle they are almost unconscious. When you can identify your assumptions it becomes a lot easier.

For instance, whenever I started cooking and slicing onions my partner always came and took the knife out of my hand and started to do it himself. It made me so mad, he made me feel like a five-year-old who could not be trusted to cut up their own food without hurting themselves. I suffered in silence, getting more and more annoyed until one day I just blew up. I started screaming and shouting about not being incapable and being able to cut things up myself and being a grown up now. He was stunned. He looked at me and said, "Of course you're not incapable, of course I know you can do it, I just don't like to see you cry." Ooops.

You see, his action pressed a button from my childhood. I had cut myself when I was young and mum refused to let me have a knife again for a year or more, so I felt as if I was being made helpless. What was really happening was that he was protecting himself from any helpless feelings he may have had for not being able to stop my tears. So he did something to ensure he would not have to see me cry. Now of course I know he does not think or feel I am stupid, I realise they were all my feelings and that I don't have to feel them anymore.

So the moral of this story is, notice when you make an assumption and check it out, for it may not be what you think it is.

When working with the throat chakra, you are working towards being able to listen to your soul and hear your own truth as well as being able to express that truth. This will take many months and years to accomplish, most probably the whole journey of life, because it keeps changing as we grow.

CHAPTER 10

Zagzagel

Brow Chakra– the Third Eye (five)

The brow chakra is about intuition, balancing the masculine and feminine energies within you. It is associated with the pituitary gland and the brain. This chakra is where you clear out old illusions so you can find your inner clarity and wisdom. As you do this you also develop your psychic skills. Don't expect to become an internationally acclaimed psychic just by going through these exercises. They are a beginning but the more you practice and clear yourself the more your intuition will develop and you'll have access not only to your own higher self and wisdom but also to the angels. The clarity with which you begin to see, hear and sense, them will increase with time.

Archangel Zagzagel

The angel who will be helping you develop your intuition is Archangel Zagzagel, angel of wisdom, compassion and inner listening. Notice if there is anything you are particularly resisting, if so give it extra attention, let go with the mind and allow Zagzagel to give you a symbol or a word to help you understand. Ask him to fill you with a deep inner knowing of your true worth or path at this time.

This is learning to listen to yourself and your own guidance coming from your guardian angel, spirit guides and your higher self. This information comes through in many ways:

Clairvoyantly – clear seeing, visions, pictures, images in your mind's eye,

Clairaudiently – clear hearing, voices in your head (don't tell your doctor!)

Clairsentiently – clear sensing, feelings in your body, maybe even physical pain or through Claircogniscence – clear thinking, ideas just pop into your head.

You can ask Archangel Zagzagel to help you hear your inner voice, whether it comes through as a voice in your mind, even sounding like your own voice, or whether it comes through your body, or your mind's eye. We don't usually listen to our bodies but it's our body that is our direct link to the divine, to our own creativity. Our bodies can't lie to us. Unlike our mind, which is everything we have learned, our body is how we experience our lives via our physical feelings. Feelings rush round the body uncontrolled by us, just like adrenaline, and as you learn to notice these feelings then so you learn your inner communication. This is clairsentience.

Intuition, Balance, Masculine and Feminine

When we are born we have a full connection to both sides of the brain, the masculine left brain, which deals with logic and learning, and the feminine right brain, which is the creative, intuitive side. In childhood they seem to be balanced and we have much fun creating new ideas, using our imagination to be so many different things and we enjoy so many different experiences. One minute you are Superman, next a knight in shining armour, next a princess, next a butterfly. Then we go to school and we have to learn to work hard. There is very little emphasis in education for creativity. We learn by rote.

With the development of the brow chakra we begin to readdress this balance and come back to trusting our intuition. The brow chakra is all about opening your inner vision. It governs the eyes, ears and nose, as well as the brain. So it's about noticing and balancing the two hemispheres of the brain. Left – masculine, logical, learned behaviour patterns, and the right – feminine, creative, intuitive, inner knowing, connection to your higher self, guides and angels. More of this later.

The issues of the brow chakra are related to the issues of the sacrum chakra because they are connected. What you are doing in this chakra is going to deeper levels and seeing things in a different way because this is all about seeing things clearly, without the fog.

I have chosen to work with Archangel Zagzagel for this chapter because of his wisdom and compassion and we are focusing on our inner wisdom in this chapter. But you can work with any of the angels associated with the brow or the sacrum chakra because these two chakras work together. Sometimes if the sacrum is so blocked, energy can be taken through the brow to bring issues into consciousness. It is entirely up to you. You can also combine the angels as we did with the throat chakra.

Brow Chakra

Location	Centre of the forehead, above and between the eyes.
Colour	Indigo Blue
Developmental Age	21 + (though sometimes never)
Sense	Insight
Glands / organs	Pituitary gland, eyes, nose, ears.
Concerns	Intuition, inspiration, confusion, clarity.
Out of balance	Lack of trust in intuition, inability to let go of logic, nightmares, conversely, always in another world.
Body symptoms	Tension headaches, migraine, visual problems, sinusitis.
Qualities / lessons	Soul realisation, imagination, clairvoyance, concentration, peace of mind, wisdom, devotion, insight, perception beyond duality.
Positive qualities	Imagination, vision, intuition, knowledge, oneness, wisdom, self-realisation.
Soul Issue	To trust the insight and intuition that comes from the perspective of your soul. To see beyond everyday limitations.
Element	None
Gems & Minerals	Amethyst, alexandrite, azurite, Herkheimer diamond, quartz crystal, lapis lazuli, sapphire, sodalite, tourmaline, tanzanite.
Associated Angels	Archangel Uriel, Archangel Gabriel, Archangel Jophiel, Archangel Zagzagal.

Associated Oils	Rose geranium, basil, black pepper, carrot seed, clary sage, clove bud, ginger, melissa (true), peppermint, pine, rosemary, rosewood, violet.

At this level we are developing our inner knowing, our inner seeing. So try this little exercise.

Choose something that is troubling you right now. It can be anything. A work problem, if you like. It does not need to be big. Perhaps something you have been thinking about for a while.

Write about it in your journal. Just the outline of what you have been thinking about.

Then, when you are ready, take your attention to your third eye, brow centre, and imagine your third eye opening. See your third eye open in your mind's eye (the space behind your forehead). Now review the situation again. What do you see differently this time?

Intuition

Everyone has some experience of intuition, knowing who is going to be on the end of the telephone when it rings, for instance. What we need to do now is to develop this inner knowing. At the brow it is about balancing intuition with gut feeling. Ensuring the gut feelings are real and not a reaction to a deep underlying fear. Getting to know your inner wisdom and most of all learning to trust it. Later there will be some exercises to do this. There are many books written about developing your intuition and I will recommend one at the end.

Clairvoyance, Clairaudience, Clairsentience, Claircogniscence

These all mean, clear seeing, clear hearing, clear sensing, and clear thinking, in that order. These are the skills you develop as you go deeper into connecting with your inner vision, your inner senses and wisdom.

Here is an exercise to help you develop your clairvoyance – clear seeing. Try practicing seeing energy and auras. You may find you do this already. Do you notice that whenever you are bored, you just stare gently into space. Well, instead stare gently at someone or something, look past the object with a gentle gaze and let your vision soften. What do you see? Just like you would if you were doing one of those 3D pictures where there is a picture amongst a load of colored dots.

As you practice you'll begin to see first an outline of energy around someone and later the colors in their auras. It takes time and practice, of course. If you don't see color with your eyes open, try closing your eyes. I often find that after I have been staring for a while if I close my eyes I get an image of the outline of the person I have been staring at which is in color. This is the predominant color of their aura.

Connecting to your Inner Vision with Archangel Zagzagel

To receive wisdom, quiet your mind and learn how to listen to your innermost being. The best way to do this is with meditation. But first decide what it is you need to ask yourself, which area of your life you wish to focus on.

So relax, focus on your breathing until you bring yourself to a deep meditative state, open and protected. Go up to the fifth dimension by pressing your thumb and fingers together, you are very good at it by now, and invoke Archangel Zagzagel to be with you by saying his name three times. Imagine yourself surrounded by a purple violet light. Feel his energy all around you. Ask him to open your brow chakra and to allow you to develop your inner vision, your creativity and inner joy.

See in your mind's eye your third eye opening and looking back at you. This usually appears in purple or gold but whatever color it is, is just right for you.

Begin to focus on your question. Messages come in many ways, sometimes through the mind as words, but usually in the form of symbols that you see, or imaginings, or sudden thoughts, or feelings and a deep knowing. You may not always receive what you want to hear.

The inner voice maybe leading you back to your true path, if you have strayed, and you need to acknowledge this then it is done with love and peace. Like, for instance, the messages your minor ailments are trying to say to you. If you are honest with yourself, you'll realise you have heard the voice for a long time and you know you have been putting it off for many years, but the time is coming when you shall have to deal with it, especially now it is appearing in your body, if you want to remain fit and healthy. Talk to Zagzagel and allow yourself to feel his inner knowing and love. Ask him to show you whatever you need to know right now for your highest good.

Then ask Zagzagel to help you express these feelings on paper. So staying with the energy, take up your journal, colouring pens, and express this energy creatively in whichever way is right for you. A picture, a poem, a song, whatever feels right to you right now. Experience the joy and certainty of inner knowing and your own creative skills. When you have finished put your book down and thank Archangel Zagzagel for his help.

Know that you can ask for his help with inner knowing at any time in the future. Or your could ask Archangel Jophiel, angel of creativity and joy, for help and inspiration with anything you are doing which is creative. Another time you could ask Jophiel to help you identify your creative talents and to assist you with expressing them, whatever they may be... ideas, art, writing, dance, sport, and remember they need not be perfect or even good, just fun and joyful for you, for your own pleasure. But know that they will improve with practice and with Archangel Jophiel's help. Enjoy the feelings for as long as you wish.

Then begin to see Archangel Zagzagel fading into the distance, knowing that you can return and bring Zagzagel or Jophiel to you again at any time in the future. Gently bring yourself back into the room, remembering to close down and protect yourself and capture your experiences in your journal.

CHAPTER 11

Melchisadec

Crown Chakra (seven)

We have worked through the third dimensional chakras in our journey so far. But as you progress and continue you'll find the colours fading and becoming crystalline then opalescent as they change and transmute, as you become a clearer and clearer channel and enhance your connection with the divine. At the throat chakra we worked with sound and toning, at the crown chakra we work with the rainbow of all colour.

You have been working through all of your issues within the chakras and letting go of whatever you don't need in this lifetime; cleansing yourself with color. You are now ready to go on to the Crown Chakra and connect to Melchisadec (Mel-kis-ah-dec) the angel prince of peace, light and spirituality. This is the master angel for spiritual awakening and wholeness.

With your crown chakra open and functioning fully you are completely connected to the universe and the divine creator. Melchisadec works specifically with the violet ray that transforms illusion and lights the way to your heart centre. He is renowned for using all the colors of the rainbow. So far we have used the colors individually, but now we shall use the whole rainbow spectrum.

Our focus in this chapter is on becoming aware of your life's purpose. Your soul's purpose since it first incarnated. What was your soul's original purpose, how are you expressing it in this lifetime, what quality is it you are looking to express in this lifetime, what is blocking you and what you need to do to remove the block? Big stuff.

Later I will also give you details of other angels you can work with as you go through the exercises as often as you wish. Each angel has its own energy and will help you at different times of your life as you let go of more and move along your life's journey.

Crown Chakra

Location	Crown, top of head
Colour	Violet, amethyst, silver, gold
Developmental Age	This chakra is open in newborns and young children, (fontanel). It can open again as a spiritual adult. It is said that the soul leaves the body through the crown chakra after death, although in Eastern and Egyptian philosophies it is thought to be through the heart chakra.
Sense	None
Glands / organs	Pineal, cerebral cortex, central nervous system, right eye.
Concerns	Knowing the unknowable, connection with the divine.
Out of balance	Despair, no sense of connection to a higher power.
Body symptoms	Depression, Parkinson's disease, epilepsy, senile dementia, brain disorders.
Qualities / lessons	The joining of higher self with the personality. Unification of higher self with the personality. Unity, Oneness with the infinite, inspiration, divine wisdom and understanding, spiritual will. Idealism, selfless service to others (Mother Teresa), perception beyond time and space, continuity of consciousness.
Negative qualities	Lack of inspiration, confusion, depression, alienation, hesitation to serve, senility.
Positive qualities	Inner knowing, doing, living in peace, acceptance, being non-judgemental, balance, happiness, spiritual awareness, bliss.
Soul Issue	To become self-aware.
Element	None
Gems & Minerals	Amethyst, alexandrite, diamond, quartz crystal, purple fluorite, charoite, celestite, selenite, sugilite,
Associated Angels	Archangel Zadkiel, Zagzagel, Melchisadec, Metatron/Shekinah.
Associated Essential Oils	Frankincense, elemi, jasmine, linden blossom, neroli, rose, rosewood, cederwood, violet leaf.

Melchisadec

There is a lot written about Melchisadec, which can be found in any search of the internet. There seem to be various schools of thought on who he was in human form; a high priest of Salem (which was the original name for Jerusalem), in the time of Abraham, as mentioned in Genesis 14; or as alluded to in the Dead Sea scrolls was he one and the same with Archangel Michael and Jesus. In the Book of Enoch, Melchisadec was the child of Noah's brother. In new age circles he is thought to be the leader of the Pleiadeans, a man who had many lifetimes. Perhaps he was all or maybe none. Perhaps he has always been Melchisadec, Father of the Angels. His symbols are rainbows, chalice and bread.

What does ring true with me from my own experiences of future life progression and the cosmos, is what Doreen Virtue writes in her book *Archangels and Ascended Masters* when she tuned in and asked him herself. Melchisadec told her:

> *"I am part of the regulating program that balances and harmonises all energies. These energies are flowing continuously and form the basic structure of the universe".* Archangels & Ascended Masters by Doreen Virtue (Hay House Publishing 2003)

He also goes on to mention to Doreen Virtue that he works with colour. Angela McGerr depicts him with rainbows of color and a chalice in her *Harmony of Angel Cards* (Quadrille Publishing). My own experience has been with his rainbow colors.

As you have progressed through this course you have been using visualisation techniques and by now must be very good at them. In the next chapter we will balance all our chakras and if you have been practicing and looking into yourself you'll have seen where you needed to do more work.

This is an ongoing experience. It is not something that is completed when you have done it once. There is always day-to-day life showing you what you need to know to go to the next level and the more you go into yourself the nearer you get to your divine being and your connectedness to the divine spirit or God.

We are now going to go on a journey to meet Melchisadec, following the rainbow light to see what wisdom he has for you. The more you do all the exercises in this program, the more your crown chakra opens and the greater your experiences will be. This is where you get to astral travel – which means that eventually, given practice, you'll be able to feel your spirit leave your body and go to other realms to learn in your sleep, before returning to your body refreshed for the morning.

For now we are focusing on meeting Melchisadec and finding your soul's purpose at this time. In doing this you'll be reviewing what you have learned about yourself so far on this journey, so, if you want to look back at your notes now and get things clear in your mind then do so, but be aware that what comes to you during the meditation is what you need to go with because it will be being guided by Melchisadec and your own higher self rather than your intellect and ego of your mind.

Visualisation of your Life Purpose

If you are lighting a candle make sure it is safe. Choose one of the oils mentioned in a this chapter and some soft relaxing music. Put this on tape if you wish, remembering to leave long pauses to enable you to have time to do the work.

Relax and make yourself comfortable. You are used to this now. Breathe deeply and with your out-breaths, focus on breathing down your roots, deep into the ground and becoming more and more relaxed. With your in-breaths, open all your chakras to the highest level and feel your body vibrating at the fifth dimension. As you focus on your breathing you become more and more relaxed.

Find yourself in a beautiful place, it may be a place you know or a place in your imagination; it's a beautiful peaceful place in nature. Spend some time reviewing what you have been learning about yourself over the course of this book. What have you found out, what have you healed, how have you moved on?

(If taping leave at least 5 – 10 minutes to do this).

Go with what comes to you right now for that is what's right for you on this occasion. Imagine you had a symbol for everything you have learned so far. Sum up everything either in a symbol, a word or a colour, whatever comes is just right for you right now.

Now you notice as you sit in your beautiful place, there is a rainbow forming in the sky. This is no ordinary rainbow, it's the bridge from earth to heaven. One end of the rainbow is all around you, you are bathed in rainbow light and as you breathe in the rainbow light you feel yourself getting lighter and lighter and floating up through the colours, up and up, following whichever stream of colour is right for you right now. Up and up you go, high into the sky, you have your eyes firmly fixed upwards, up into the universe as the rainbow light carries you higher and higher into the divine realms. As you rise higher and higher you become lighter and lighter and more and more relaxed. You become happier and happier as you feel joy at being one with the rainbow of light, knowing it is taking you to meet Melchisadec, the angel of peace and spirituality, knowing that he will strip away all the illusions you have about yourself, all the ego defences, and will show you your purpose and your way forward.

Feel yourself rising along the rainbow of light and see yourself coming to a wonderful place, whatever place this is, it is the place you need to be right now. You see a mighty angel waiting for you. As you get closer it becomes clearer and clearer. Its wings merge with the rainbow light around you. What does this angel look like, what does it feel like? Notice everything there is to notice about how Melchisadec appears to you. What do you sense, what do you smell, what do you taste, what do you hear, what do you see.

(If taping leave a couple of minutes)

As you approach, feel the love and compassion and acceptance of Melchisadec. Sit and talk, listen to what Melchisadec has to say to you. How pleased he is with your journey so far. Let Melchisadec take you to the time when your soul was incarnating, see a film of yourself incarnating for the first time, what was your soul's purpose back then in that early time before you lost your way through many lifetimes? What quality was it that you were bringing to the world? Hope, love, wisdom, light, prayer, stability, creativity, fulfilment, movement, joy, happiness... And how were you going to achieve it in this lifetime. Ask Melchisadec what's blocking you right now to being that quality you first brought with you. What's your true destiny for this lifetime?

(If taping leave a couple of minutes)

As Melchisadec reveals to you your true destiny, go with Melchisadec, float out into your future and see yourself living the life of your true destiny, experience yourself in five or ten years time. How do you feel, what are you doing, what's going on in your life, far below you? Feel how happy you are, know that you have achieved your full potential and are living the life you came here to live, doing what you love, being your true self. Spend some time watching and learning from the future you.

(If taping leave a few minutes)

When you are ready look back, let Melchisadec reveal to you what's blocking you and how it can be removed to set you free to be your true divine self and achieve your life's purpose.

(If taping leave a minute)

What's your next step to enlightenment? Melchisadec is giving you a gift, it may be a symbol it may be a tool, it may be a word, whatever it is it is right for you right now. Accept the gift and thank Melchisadec for everything and start to return along the rainbow light coming back along the rainbow light back, back, back into your body and into your room. Wiggle your fingers and toes and have a drink of water.

Quickly write up your notes of this experience. What have you learned about your soul's journey so far? What are you going to do next?

Choices and Indecisiveness

At many times in our lives we have to make choices and most of us can be indecisive. This is often because we are trying too hard to get it right. We are thinking hard with our minds, often driving ourselves crazy going round and round in circles, and not listening to our gut reactions and our body.

Our body can't lie to us. Unlike our minds, which are full of learned behaviour, both from our own experience, our family values and our culture, our bodies have direct communication with our higher selves and the creative universe. This is why we feel everything in our body. We are here on this planet as divine beings to experience life in our human bodies. In spirit we feel nothing except love; on earth we experience our life and our soul through our body.

If you have a near accident whilst driving, or someone startles you, your body automatically produces adrenaline. You notice this as a feeling within yourself and you go into automatic response mode. Your senses then assess the extent of the danger and you act accordingly. Sometimes this has happened so fast you have not even had time to think, sometimes your instincts join forces with your mind but normally at times like this you follow your instincts – is it safe, or is it time for flight, fight or freeze.

The same is true when making decisions, your body will have the answer to what's best for you. What you choose to do with this information is then up to you. For instance, you are not sure if you want to leave your job, relationship, what new career might be best for you. Whatever the question, whatever the choice, become aware that you have choice. The choice always remains your own so be aware that if you choose to follow your lack of energy it is your choice and not because you can't do the opposite.

Be aware, if you say to yourself things like, "I can't do that until the children grow up", or "my spouse won't let me", that you are making an unconscious choice to do nothing. That's OK as long as you are aware it's your choice, that you are powerful in making that choice, not helpless because you are not making a choice.

As you have been working through the exercises in this book you'll have reached the stage where you are much more aware of the physical sensations in your body and how your body speaks to you. For after all, your spirit resides in your body not your mind and speaks to you through it. This is why the body is often referred to as the 'temple of the soul'.

Many of us can be very indecisive, though often in only one area of our lives. For instance, you may easily be able to make decisions at work but find it very difficult to make decisions around yourself, like, should I change my job? Should I stay with my partner?

Now you are more aware of the physical feelings in your body, I can show you a quick way to find out what your soul actually wants you to do because it will speak to you through your body. It will put energy in some way or other into the decision that is right for you and if you make a decision that is right for you it will be right for everyone else concerned as well. This is a physical response that is out of your mental control, like adrenaline being pumped into your system in an emergency, so your body will have some type of physical reaction. By learning to notice it you'll also be able to know what is right for you. What you do with that knowledge is then up to you.

You can do the following exercise when you have a number of alternatives, just give yourself the options and always put things in the positive. Whichever choice has energy, whatever carries a feeling rather than lethargy or depression, is the choice that is right for you.

For this example think of a decision you may have to make between three alternatives; let's call them A, B and C. Say to yourself :

"I am going to do A" …
How does it feel? What's happening to your body?
Are your shoulders sagging?
Do you feel lethargic?

Does it seem like a sensible solution?
Do you feel any energy in this statement?

Then say to yourself:
"I am going to do B" ...

"I am going to do C" ... How does that feel?
Do you have butterflies in your tummy?
Do you feel something? Is it fear or excitement? (They actually both feel the same, it is your choice what you choose it to be.)
Does your mind start thinking about how you could do it, or even why you can't?
Have your eyes lit up?
Are you sitting more straight in your chair, or standing more upright?
Are you trying not to smile?
Are you trying not to feel terrified?

There you have your answer. You have energy in this choice.

What you do with this is then up to you. You can start thinking about why this is the best option, because when your mind and your body agree there is no problem making a decision you just know. Or you can ask yourself what stops you. "What do I need to do to make this decision safe for me?"If it feels overwhelming then make a list of all the reasons why you can't do this choice and start asking yourself, what stops you? Work backwards until you find what it is. Often it goes back to a lack of confidence or not enough knowledge. What would you need to do next to become more confident, gain more knowledge?

For instance, if you were thinking of leaving your partner but one of the things on your list was that you had no where to go. What would you need to do to find somewhere? Perhaps you have no money so you would need to find a job first. Just keep working backwards until you find something you can begin to do.

Or if you are thinking of changing your career and don't know what you want to do, perhaps you could see a career counsellor or just give yourself permission to spend the next year attending different workshops or taking evening classes and see what you actually enjoy doing.

See what works for you. As long as you can find one thing where you can take positive action you'll be taking responsibility and control of your life. It may take time but that's fine, you can still choose to take the first option for now, but you know that you are working towards what's right for you and that's what's important.

The first action may be as simple as getting a book out of the library to find out more. Whatever you do is fine, because what's important is changing the energy from negative to positive. With every positive step you take then all the other obstacles start to change as well. As the age old riddle goes: "how do you eat an elephant?" answer: "one mouthful at a time". So break down any problems into small manageable steps. Then watch over your shoulder and see all the steps you have taken. One average step is two feet, the next and the next and before you know it you have travelled the first mile then the next.

If you wanted to win a gold medal for swimming at the Olympics the first thing you would need to do is learn to swim. When you have done that you have achieved something that you had not done before. That's your success. Then you join a swimming club and practice, practice, practice. You get better and better and better and you begin to feel more confident. Wherever you get to you have done more than before. It is not the result that matters so much as being in the game of life. The journey of life is one small step at a time.

You are the only one who will judge your life on your death bed and however many lives you have had, or will have, you only have this one, this particular minute, right now, once, so experience it to the full. Good and bad. We are often so afraid of feeling bad feelings like fear or sadness that we forget that the opposite is excitement and joy and those feelings when experienced in the body can be both at the same time. How we choose to experience them is up to us. For instance, when a child leaves home to go to university or to marry we are sad and in pain because we miss them, a part of our life has come to an end, but we are joyful for them, and we can choose to be joyful for ourselves because this means there can be a new and exciting beginning for us as well.

Quite often we fear the future, the unknown and we have difficulty leaving what we know and taking those risks. We can, and do, choose whether we find this experience to be fearful and helpless or exciting and powerful. This is our choice. Things end and things begin, that is the cycle of life, we can't change it, but we can choose how we experience it. Transform your life from fear-based to power-based.

Letting go of Addictions with Archangel Uriel

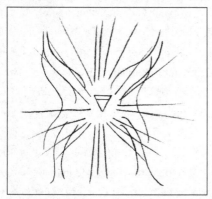

All the angels can be used to help you let go of addictions, because all the angels bring healing in their own right as well as their own particular quality. It is not just Archangel Raphael who brings healing. I have chosen to work with Archangel Uriel in this instance because of the determination he brings with him and for most of us when trying to give something up, it's our willpower and determination that needs strengthening, whether it be types of food, alcohol, drugs, cigarettes, addictive relationships, or even specific behaviour such as nail biting or negative traits such as being stubborn. You can also work with Archangel Micah. It is easy to have the intention and to start but it's not always easy to keep at it and to complete it. As you continue with this work in the future you can use other angels to assist you in letting go of other addictions if you wish.

Having decided which addiction you wish to let go of, relax and centre yourself. Invoke Archangel Uriel to be with you, as you did in the previous exercise. Feel his energy with you.

Then imagine the addiction as a separate entity in front of you, let it take on a form or a colour, it may be a black blob, or a stone, or a jellyfish. Whatever it is – it's just right for you. Imagine the cords that tie this addiction to you. See them, what are they made of, how big are they, how many of them are there, see and feel yourself connected to this addiction.

In your imagination talk to the addiction, ask what its positive purpose is for you, what is it trying to achieve, what is it protecting you from? Allow yourself to become aware of its positive intention.

Ask Archangel Uriel if there is another way this intention can be achieved and if so how, or, whether this intention is actually positive for you, whether it is for your highest good at this time in your life or whether it's an outdated belief or inherited belief? Listen to what Archangel Uriel has to say. Continue your dialogue with your addiction and Uriel until you reach an acceptable solution. Ask what might be needed to allow it to let go.

(If you are putting this on tape leave 5 minutes here)

When you have reached a solution, allow Uriel to dissolve the cords of the addiction, with his gold or purple light, healing any wounds. See and feel the cords dissolving, disappearing one by one. See the addiction free and clear of you – no longer connected in any way – and ask Uriel to transmute all and any negativity energy from the addiction into positive energy for your highest good.

Ask Archangel Uriel if there is anything else you'll need to allow you to let go of this addiction once and for all. If there is allow yourself to know what these are and to accept them into your life. Ask Uriel to surround you with love and determination and then allow yourself to visualise the addiction getting smaller and smaller and paler and paler until it has vanished into the either and no longer exists.

When you feel you have finished, thank Archangel Uriel for his help and gently come back into the room. Have a drink of water and write your experiences in your journal.

Balancing Masculine and Feminine Energies with Metatron and Shekinah

Everyone has both masculine and feminine energy and it is important to balance these energies within each and every one of us. There is a very

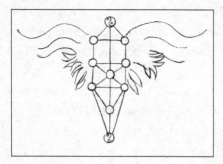

simple technique with which we can do this.

Metatron and Shekinah are one and the same and separate. It is said that Shekinah is the feminine aspect of God and Metatron the masculine aspect of God. They sit at the top of the tree of life just as Ariel and Sandolphon sit at the bottom. I often think of Shekinah as being the hidden feminine energy of men, with Metatron as the masculine energy of women.

This is a very short and powerful visualization to balance and grow these energies within yourself.

Relax and focus on your breathing. By now you are familiar with bringing earth energy up from the ground through your feet and in bringing universal energy down from above. Know that earth energy is feminine and universal energy is masculine.

As you focus on your breathing and breath these energies into your heart, see and sense them combine. However you sense, feel or see these energies is just right for you but you could imagine them as silver and gold threads entwining themselves around each other forming a stronger and stronger thread like thin unbreakable rope. As they spin themselves more and more tightly together see, sense and feel the threads opening up and know the molecules, the DNA of each of these energies are opening to each other and fusing together forming a new and stronger DNA chain, our original divine DNA. See the original blue print of the divine being reborn in your DNA. Feel all your strands of DNA opening to this combined energy. Feel the fusing of the masculine and feminine energies within you. Fusing together and bring you balance. Let this energy flow round your body. Sense the ancient pathways of logic and intuition being reopened within your being so they can blend together. Breathe this into your head, in your heart, into every cell of your being. See, sense and feel this new balanced energy flowing through your body and your mind, bringing peace and balance within you. Allowing you to access all your divine self and allowing you to bring it into your everyday life to take you forward along your soul's path. Enjoy this feeling for as long as you wish, and when ready slowly bring yourself back into your room.

CHAPTER 12

Other Angels

Throughout the journey there have been other angels mentioned within the chakra tables. You can work with these at any time. Every angel's energy will be different and each angel will give you a further insight into your current issues at each level of the chakras. Go with the flow, follow your intuition, which will be much more developed now – whichever angel attracts your attention at any particular time will be the one you need to be working with at that time. As you continue working with the angels and healing yourself then so your intuition and psychic powers will develop and so you can chose to use them in your life and if you wish to help others.

The Pentagram of Angels

The pentagram of angels will help you discover which of the major 22 angels are working with you now. It will enable you to focus on particular aspects of your life and encourage you gently along your spiritual pathway. A full colour version and additional information on the other angels is available on my website at www.joylina.com

How to Use the Pentagram of Angels

Sit in a comfortable position with the picture in front of you. Close your eyes and relax. Become aware of your breathing. Take a few deep breaths inhaling love and light and exhaling all your stress, tension and negativity.

Place your left hand palm down about 3 inches above over the picture and draw a figure 8 with your hand over it 11 times to put your energy into the pentagram. Then asking for guidance from the angels as to which particular which angel is waiting to help you right now in any area of your life. If you have a pendulum or other form of dowser and wish to dowse then just hold it 4-6 inches above the picture and slowly let it move over the different angels names. As soon as it starts to move, you have your angel.

Keeping your eyes closed, allow your hand to hover over the page, and ask a specific question or for general guidance.

Allow a finger to point down so it is pointing towards the picture and move your finger over the diagram, sensing if you are drawn to any particular area and then gently allow your finger rest on the page.

Open your eyes and see which angel or angels are helping you now. Much of the information you'll need to guide you is in this book but your own intuition and imagination is how your angels will be communicating to you. So always follow what your intuition and your body are saying to you. Remember that your mind (logic) can mislead you, so follow what feels right to you.

When you have finished consulting the angels place your hand palm down on the diagram again to thank the angels for their guidance and blessings.

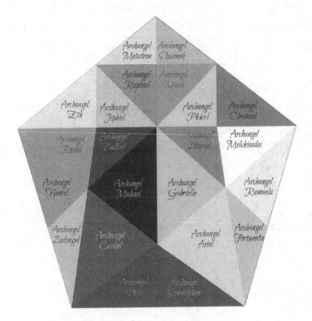

Pentagram of Angels

Extra exercises

Other Techniques You Can Use for Balancing and Clearing Any Chakras

How Do You Know When You Are Blocked

This actually applies to any of the chakras depending upon your symptoms. If you find you are suffering from an ailment look to see what part of your body it is affecting.

For instance, whilst writing this book I have noticed many things and I still go deeper into my own clearing. I noticed I had a very raspy throat. Then my sinuses joined in. This told me that something was not quite right, especially on the throat chakra.

Perhaps there's an area of my life where I'm not being honest with myself and speaking up. When my sinuses joined in perhaps there is something I'm not looking at clearly? Or am I seeing what I want to see and ignoring my deep inner vision and knowing. (I'm still very good at that). The questions I have to ask myself are, what is blocking me? What am I not noticing in my life or trying to ignore? Is it because it's going to be so difficult to accomplish? If I face my deepest fears I know in myself what it is and what I need to do, but I am avoiding it. Hence all the minor dis-eases coming out in my body because my mental, emotional, physical, spiritual selves are out of balance.

Seeing and balancing is what this is all about. So continue to balance your chakras whenever you can – preferably daily. The more you create your experience in your imagination, (which is using your right feminine intuitive brain), the more clearly you'll be able to see your future, what your underlying needs are, what you need to let go of.

There are many exercises you can do to help release any blockages in your chakras.

Visualisation with Light

Firstly sit and relax and open your chakras and protect yourself. Then look objectively at each chakra. What colours are they, are they clear and bright, are they all the same size, are some smaller than others, are some sluggish. Whatever they are like is OK. Don't judge yourself. Then using a clear white light or whatever feels right for you, just give your chakras a spring clean, clear them out, make them all bright and crystal clear, make them all the same size, breathe into each one and make it larger or smaller until they are all the same size and brightness. Notice how much better you feel. You can do this whenever you want, most people do it every day and as you get more experienced it does not take much time you can do it in the shower, whilst cleaning your teeth, whenever. As you progress you'll notice the colour stays brighter and the size of the chakras get bigger and bigger.

Toning

Toning is a great way to help clear your chakras. You can focus on any chakra and just allow your mouth to open and a note to come out. Take a deep breath before you do this because you want to hold the tone as long as possible. Tone each note three times. What you'll find is that quite automatically you'll tone a different note for each chakra, and when you have been through each chakra, focus on your inner being and tone the note of your soul.

This can be a really rewarding and soulful experience. You don't have to be a good singer. You can do this in the privacy of your own home when no one is around but don't judge your voice. (If you really don't like the sound of your own voice imagine one of the angels toning for you.) When you do this toning you'll notice that it makes a really beautiful sound.

Increasing Confidence

Everything we have been doing through this journey will have been increasing your confidence in yourself. But there is a way, which is very quick and simple, for you to boost your confidence in any particular area of your life. We will be combining a number of NLP techniques for this.

Firstly make yourself comfortable and relaxed. Imagine a circle in front of you. The circle can be any colour whatever you need right now. Don't step into the circle just see it in front of you. Now I want you to think about the particular instance you want to feel confident for. Perhaps it is a job interview, perhaps a sporting event, whatever it is, just bring it to mind.

Now go back to a time in your life when you felt confident about something. If it is related to the event in your mind at present, so much the better, but it does not need to be. Anything you achieved, anything you did well and were praised for. Go back into your memory (it does not matter which area of your life it is, any will do). Remember and allow yourself to experience those feelings of confidence in your body again. See yourself, what are you wearing, how are you standing, sitting, what are you doing, how are you feeling, what can you smell? Make it a big bright picture in your mind of you feeling supremely confident. When your picture in your mind is as big and beautiful as you can make it then I want you to step into the circle.

Now I want to you imagine what else you might need to make yourself feel even more confident. What are the qualities and skills you need that others might possess? Are there people who are particularly good at the skills you want to exhibit? What might you benefit from to make yourself feel even more confident? Is there anyone you like and admire who has the quality of confidence in this particular circumstance that you can copy? How do they stand, what do they do? See yourself the same way. Start to bring all the qualities, skills, items etc into the circle with you, whatever is appropriate to each individual need. Now notice how you begin to feel even more confident.

Don't worry about what comes in just bring in whatever you need. Most people bring their childhood teddy bear or comforter, as well as personalities both dead and alive. It does not matter what it is as long as it increases your confidence. If it's a business matter maybe I want Richard Branson or Bill Gates or both, if I was going to stand up a sing perhaps I would like Maria Callas or Madonna, if I was going to paint a picture perhaps I'd want Michaelangelo. Get the idea! Certainly I always want the angels in my circle.

Make the picture even bigger and sunnier, noisier, calmer whatever is right for you to feel supremely confident. When you have made it as fantastic as you can anchor, these feelings on your body in some way. Perhaps making a fist with your hand, perhaps a noise, or an action. Many people do all three, eg. make a tight fist, punch the air saying "yes" or whatever is appropriate to you. I stand still and calm, take a deep breath in close my eyes, breathe in the peace, love and confidence of my guides and angels and say to myself "Come on team, we're on", and I know I will succeed at whatever I am undertaking then.

Spiritual Growth

There are lessons and experiences that we have agreed to have either from a karmic point of view or from a soul growth point of view. Both are equally relevant. We come to experience being ourselves and our inter-relationships with other souls.

As we journey into ourselves we become closer to our soul and to God, the universe and everything. We are a part of everything. We are energy, and energy is everything. God is energy. In Neale Donald Walsch's book *Conversations with God* he speaks about us being fragments of God. He says God fragmented himself so he/she could experience itself.

It's my belief that our whole lives are a journey to experience our soul within the environment of a human body. Spiritual growth is a journey that takes a lifetime or many lifetimes. We are constantly growing closer to ourselves. The more we explore and express our true natures, the more we connect to the unconditional love within us, the happier we and our world will be.

This whole book has been a journey of spiritual growth. If you have worked through all the exercises you are well on your way to self-enlightenment. Life itself is your spiritual growth. Remember you continue to grow and evolve through every day and every experience right up until you pass from this world to the next, where you'll continue the process in another form, before you reincarnate and continue the journey. Every moment is the beginning of the rest of your life, so chose wisely how to spend right now. The journey always starts here.

Conclusion

Well I hope you have enjoyed your journey with the angels through your chakras and have found a way that you can bring not only the angels energy into your life but also to find a closer relationship to yourself and your spiritual path.

This is not a once in a lifetime journey. These exercises will help you throughout the rest of life, as you continue the journey deeper and deeper into knowing your true self, releasing your fears and living the life you came here to live. With the angels in your life you will never be lonely, you will never fear doing the wrong thing and you'll always know that you are loved and cherished and guided through your journey of life.

Life is for living, for enjoying and finding fulfillment. It is not to be rushed, as fast as possible down the freeway but to be explored and learned from, taking every side turning and cart track to every beautiful place we have in our physical world and in our spiritual world. Enjoying and learning from every meal and experience along the way. If you let the Angels light your path for you it will become easy and exhilarating, joyous and fun and you will be a light and a beacon for others to follow.

Remember it's the journey, that's important, not the destination.

FURTHER READING

The Book of Angels (Within the Gold & Silver Guardian Angels Set) Angela McGerr (Quadrille Publishing, 2004)

The Rainbow Journey Dr Brenda Davies (Coronet Books, Hodder & Stoughton, 1998)

Your Body Speaks Your Mind Debbie Shapiro (Piatkus, 1996)

Soulwork Sue Minns (Light Publishing, 1997)

Angel Therapy Denise Whichello Brown (D & S Books, 2001)

A Little Light on Angels Diana Cooper (Findhorn Press, 1996)

Angels A – Z ~ A Who's Who of the Heavenly Host Matthew Bunson (Three Rivers Press, New York, 1996)

Know Your Angels John Ronner, (Mamre Pres, 1993)

Archangels & Ascended Masters Doreen Virtue (Hay House Publishing, 2003)

The Fragrant Mind Valerie Ann Worwood (Doubleday)

Frontiers of Health – From Healing to Wholeness Dr Christine R Page (CW Daniel Co)

Dreams ~ A Portal to the Source Edward C Whitmont & Silivia Brinton Perera, (Brunner-Routledge, 1989)

Grace Unfolding Greg Johanson and Ron Kurtz (Bell Tower New York, 1991)

The Hero Within ~ 6 Archetypes We Live By Carol S Peason PH.D. (Harper San Francisco, 1986)

What We May Be Piero Ferrucci (Thorsons, 1982)

Sub-Personalities ~ The People Inside Us John Rowan (Routledge, 1990)

The Soul's Code James Hillman (Bantam Books, 1996)

Care of the Soul Thomas Moore (Piatkus, 1992)

Conversations with God Neale Donald Walsch (Hay House)

The NLP Coach Ian McDermott and Wendy Jago (Piatkus, 2001)

The Tibetan Book of Living and Dying Sagyal Rinpoche (Harper San Francisco, 1992)

Recommended Music

Return of the Angels Philip Chapman (New World Music, 1991)
Angels Llewellyn (New World Music, 2002)
Temple in the Forest (Valley of the Sun Publishing, 1982)
Resonation of Angels Neil H (Neil H Music, 2002)
Angel Love Aeoliah (Oreade Music, 1999)

Visualisation CDs

Your Angel Journey CDs – available at www.joylina.com
Tuning In to Spirit Guides & Angels with Joylina available at www.joylina.com

Angel Cards

Gold & Silver Guardian Angels Set & the Book of Angels Angela McGerr (Quadrille)
Heart & Soul Angel Cards Angela McGerr (Quadrille)
Harmony Angel Cards Angela McGerr (Quadrille)
Angels of Light Diana Cooper
The Angels Script Theolyn Cortens – The Souls School – 2004
Healing with Angels Doreen Virtue (Hay House Publishing)

To contact Joylina

Email: joylina@joylina.com
or see her website: www.joylina.com